ENDORSEMENTᴸ

Andy Elmes' new book, Soul Winner, *takes a fresh look at effective evangelism in the world today. He has put together a practical guide for all who desire to personally bring people to Jesus. Elmes shares key elements of witnessing, how to navigate the harvest field, and most importantly, how to lead people to the Lord! This book is a compass for the go-getters, equipping them with everything they must know, to be successful soul winners for the kingdom of God!*

Daniel Kolenda
President and CEO of Christ for All Nations;

This book will circumnavigate the world. It will be found on trains in Europe, busses in Argentina, boats in the Atlantic. It will be found on coffee tables in corporate offices, on bedside tables in neighbourhoods. It will be carried in the sweaty hands of third world evangelists, strapped to the carriers of African bicycles. It will be read on planes, taxis and ferries. It will be carried across the Himalayas, the Andes, and the Atlas Mountains. It will be found on the cloud of social media and quoted from the pulpits of the world. Pages of this book will be torn out and sent out to congregations to circulate between people, and the fingerprints of kings and emperors, subjects and peasants, will be found on these pages, translated into many languages.

All this, because the dream of God is that every person on earth discover His love, grace and redemption. This book – in the hands of the faithful gospel witness – is a gateway through which God's dream will be realised.

For thus saith the LORD of hosts; Yet once, it is a little while, and I will shake the heavens, and the earth, and the sea, and the dry land; And I will shake all nations, and the desire of all nations shall come: and I will fill this house with glory, saith the LORD of hosts. (Haggai 2:6-7)

Philip Smethurst
President and founder of Overland Missions.

In a world where fake news, half-truths and confusion often exists, what a privilege to have the one news that changed the world when it arrived and continues to change lives today. The Gospel is truly the greatest of Good News! If ever there was a moment in time for the church of God to embrace the mandate to proclaim Christ, this is it. Times of turbulence require action, for if fear brings paralysis, Gospel action is the antidote.

I read a book entitled Soul Winner *over thirty years ago – CH Spurgeon, of course, penned it. In it, he says "Every man here, every woman here, every child here whose heart is right with God, may be a soul-winner." What declaration, what encouragement! You can win souls for Christ!*

Andy Elmes has been a friend for over twenty years. In that time, Andy has fine-tuned and worked through the principles of soul-winning found within this book in a way that means this manuscript is not theory, it's fool proof. It works! Do you have friends and family who need Jesus? Does your heart burn with a desire to see not only them but your community and nation turn to Jesus too? Then you simply have to read this book. Applying the tools in this book matters: why? Because both Heaven and Hell await the outcome! Get to it, dear reader – eternity is waiting.

Glyn Barrett
Assemblies of God Great Britain National Leader/Empowered21 Western Europe Co-chair and Lead Pastor of Audacious Church.

At the beginning of 2020, no one could have seen that in just a few short months, the world would be severely impacted by a global pandemic. As the UK lockdown took effect, church buildings closed, services moved online, and many wondered how the UK Church would cope. Even here at UCB, while we are used to fast-moving technology, repositioning our team to work remotely, in the space of twenty-four hours, presented its own unique challenges. But not only have we thrived and seen a huge demand for our resources, but I have also been delighted to see the global Church respond in fresh and innovative ways too. Andy's new book is a reflection on how we as believers can harness this newfound enthusiasm and energy and use it to reach our world. We see all around us that 'the fields are white' and so Soul Winner *is a call to action, offering simple but effective ways to reach more people. From a concise explanation of the doctrine of salvation (for those who want to really understand the message) to thoughts on how to start a conversation with a non-believer, Andy's book contains some great wisdom as well as practical tips on how to make an impact.*

The message of the Gospel hasn't changed, but the way we share it has. While we 'weep with those who weep', we also know that the Church was born for a time just like this. As you read this book, allow it to challenge and inspire you, to a new level of faith and action.

David L'Herroux
Chief Executive of United Christian Broadcasting Europe.

Andy is my brother and a fellow pastor. When we get together, we inevitably get talking about what we are each learning, and it is amazing how often we discover that God has been speaking to us both along similar lines. Last time it was all about the call on every follower of Jesus to step into the harvest field and to share their faith with confidence in the one who calls them. That is the heart of this book and the message that is passionately and practically delivered in its pages. Andy seeks to encourage us all to get involved with the people in our lives and to share the good news we bear, moving in the power of God, responding to each unique situation, and remembering that we are always part of the journey for others. There are lots of good stories from Andy's own life – like the one about coming across an outdoor karaoke party somewhere in the Philippines and getting roped into singing a couple of numbers, which turned into an impromptu gospel presentation! When I read this I thought, 'I could never see myself doing that!' To which Andy, I know, would reply, 'You are not meant to – rather, you bring the good (great) news in a way that only you can, drawing on your background, personality and gifts, in the power of the Holy Spirit.' That is a point Andy makes clearly – we are all uniquely equipped for this. What is crucial is that we give ourselves to joyfully sharing what (who) we know, learning as we go.

Stephen Elmes
Baptist Minister and Author of Sexuality, Faith & the Art of Conversation

SOUL WINNER
A Handbook for Lifestyle Evangelism

Everything you need to know to lead others to Jesus

Andy Elmes

Published in 2020 by Great Big Life Publishing
Empower Centre, 83-87 Kingston Road, Portsmouth, PO2 7DX, UK

British Library Cataloguing in Publication Data

A catalogue record for this book is available from the British Library.

Cover design by Matt Russell, createthatart.co.uk

ISBN-13: 978-1-9160388-6-8
eBook: 978-1-9160388-7-5

Acknowledgements

I would like to say thanks to a few people for helping to get this book written and published.

TEAM ELMES:

Massive thanks again to Gina and my kids for your patience and support. So grateful for how you allow me to get obsessed and hyper focused on projects like this and cheer me on while I am. Thank you, love you all very much, team Elmes.

OLIVIA ELMES
WILDPURSUIT.UK

Thank you, Olivia, for the many hours you poured into this book reading and repairing all of my terrible grammar and punctuation mistakes. Thank you for being so hands-on with this project, I really appreciate it. Continue to change the world, darling, one life at a time. Proud of you.

MATT RUSSELL
CREATETHATART.CO.UK

Big thanks, Matt and createthatart.co.uk, for the fantastic cover. Thank you for taking my thoughts and ideas and making a great looking cover from them, looks great, Matt, thanks.

MATT LOCKWOOD
MATTSSTUDIO.CO.UK

Big thanks again, Matt, for taking pages of my words and thoughts and laying them out in a way that people can read them in an enjoyable and easy way.

Dedication

I would like to dedicate this book to the memory of all the great soul winners who have gone before us. The men and women who gladly and passionately gave away their lives to see others find Christ and His kingdom. This list could include so many faithful men and women of God from times past, but I would like to specifically honour the memory of:

Charles Spurgeon, Charles Finney, William and Catherine Booth, George Whitefield, DL Moody, John and Charles Wesley, Jonathan Edwards, John Knox, James Hudson Taylor, Billy Graham and Reinhard Bonnke.

Thank you for leaving such a great legacy of evangelism and giving us such great examples to follow.

Contents

New Horizons

If you would have said to me at the time I started writing this book, the beginning of 2020, that in a few short months every church building in the world would be shut, their doors locked and their gates bolted because of a worldwide pandemic, I probably would have smirked at you in total disbelief! Yet that is exactly what has happened. At the time of writing this, church buildings are still closed, large gatherings are mostly illegal, and masks must be worn in public spaces. Some churches have closed their doors for good and a number of pastors have resigned, feeling that their ministries are over. I can see the difficulty of this moment; however, I also see this as a crucial moment for the Church. You see, the reality is that the Church did not shut – their buildings did! As I've said repeatedly over the years: the Church was never a building, we just met in them; the Church was never a service, we just had them. The Church always has and always will be a community of

> The Church was never a building, we just met in them; the Church was never a service, we just had them.

people who have been called out of darkness and into His light, who are filled with His life. The inconceivable moment we are currently living in is actually causing us, His Church, to re-evaluate and rediscover ourselves and our mission in a fresh and very powerful way. We are looking at ourselves in a way that we probably would not have done unless the buildings and stages that we trusted in so much had not been shut down for a time.

It was around the middle of 2019 that I began to hear the Lord say two words to me: new horizons. At first, I thought He was speaking to me about new destinations, thinking that perhaps He was giving me a new assignment. However, I quickly realised that these new horizons were not about my assignment, but rather they were about the Church at large. He was preparing us so that we would be ready for the new things that were about to happen. The Church needed to be ready for brand-new horizons of ministry, that were unlike anything we had seen or experienced before.

Naturally speaking, a horizon is the space where sky and earth seemingly meet or connect. Spiritually speaking, a horizon is the place where heaven and earth meet; where supernatural meets natural and heavenly meets human. This is what I believe the Church, or the people of God, are supposed to be. We are God's new horizon for the time we are in. Through us, God desires to minister to a lost and separated world, reconciling it back to Himself. I am reminded of the passage of scripture, Genesis 28:10-17, where Jacob had a

> A horizon is the place where heaven and earth meet; where supernatural meets natural and heavenly meets human.

16

dream at Bethel. In his dream, Jacob saw spiritual things ascending and descending in a supernatural relationship between heaven and earth. After waking up he said, "Surely this place is the house of God." What did he mean? The place where he sat was a portal where he experienced heaven touching earth. Just like that stairway created a relationship between heaven and earth, today there remains a relationship between these two realms; the point where they connect is called the Church!

There are heavenly things that God wants to do on the earth today. His plan, as it has always been since Jesus rose from the dead, is to do these things through His Church, which is His house on the earth. This house is not a building or a cathedral, rather it is us, wherever we may be. You see, we don't go to church, we are the Church! Our lives are this gateway, or place of meeting, between heaven and earth. We, the Church (the people not the building), are the new horizon; we are the point where heaven and earth interact, and God's will is revealed and released.

> Right now, there is a divine awakening taking place. All across the world God's harvesters are waking up to the fresh call that is coming from the harvest fields.

So, when God says to us that it is a time of new horizons, He is announcing that it is a *kairos* moment! A moment of divine resetting for His Church. This is a fresh moment, where we are able to see with true 20/20 vision what it is that we are on the earth to do. Right at the centre of this vision is our commission to reach lost people and to bring them back to God.

Right now, there is a divine awakening taking place. All across the world God's harvesters are waking up to the fresh call that is coming from the harvest fields. They are arising from their slumber and embracing this original mandate. This is the time for the Church to shine and to no longer be asleep in the light, as Keith Green put it so well. We are to be the light shining in the darkness that Isaiah 60 says we are destined to be; the unhidden city on a hill, and the uncovered light that Jesus referred to in Matthew 5:14-16.

Now that we are no longer hiding in our buildings, obsessed with our own spirituality and our soulish needs, maybe we can get down to real business – Kingdom business! Can you not hear the alarm clock sounding? This is the hour when the Church must arise, the saints must be equipped, and the harvesters must be sent out!

> Now that we are no longer hiding in our buildings, obsessed with our own spirituality and our soulish needs, maybe we can get down to real business – Kingdom business!

When the doors of our church buildings one day open again, we must be different! May we all, regardless of the denomination that we belong to, have a greater revelation of the actual purpose of our gatherings and an accompanying revelation of how God desires to use us, even in our scattering. A somewhat parallel moment to that which we are now in, can be seen in Acts 8:1. We see the early Church, not that long after they opened, beginning to become settled in their meetings and formats, when suddenly they were scattered throughout Judea and Samaria because of persecution. They were suddenly thrust back into the harvest field that Jesus had called them to! What would this scattering have initially felt like for those who were living in that moment? It must have been confusing, unnerving, and uncomfortable. Yet, as is promised in Romans 8:28, God was at work, even in that moment. He was working for the good of the Church and the purposes that He had for her. What seemed like a bad thing turned into a great thing! Yes, their regular gatherings had been somewhat ruined, but as a result the attendees went to the places that He had originally called them to and some set sail for the four corners of the world! As a result of this great scattering, the world was impacted. What if God is using this moment to shake His Church, to equip, and to send us into the world to reach people who we might not have considered before? What if!

> As a result of this great scattering, the world was impacted. What if God is using this moment to shake His Church, to equip, and to send us into the world to reach people who we might not have considered before? What if!

This, my friends, is indeed a *kairos* moment; a moment when the harvest is calling, "Come". As you step into the pages of this book with a heart to learn, my prayer for you is that something fresh will awaken in your heart for the lost. My hope is that you will be empowered, equipped, and sent to reach the lost.

CHAPTER 1

The Equipping of the Saints

How then shall they call on Him in whom they have not believed? And how shall they believe in Him of whom they have not heard? And how shall they hear without a preacher? And how shall they preach unless they are sent? As it is written: "How beautiful are the feet of those who preach the gospel of peace, who bring glad tidings of good things!" (Romans 10:14-15)

Good news – God has removed the separation between Himself and man. Anyone who comes through Jesus can now have a personal relationship with Him. This means that we are now able to experience the fullness of salvation and new life that He desires for us! This is, indeed, good news – but how will others know about this good news unless people are sent to tell them? This book is for every person who has the desire to see the people in their world find the same life-transforming walk with Jesus that they have found.

The subject of this book is evangelism. We will specifically focus on personal evangelism, which is also referred to as lifestyle evangelism. You see, evangelism can have a number of different expressions in the Christian life. One of these expressions is speaking to crowds at a conference, a church, or other public gathering. Another expression of evangelism is a person's individual commitment to be a witness who chooses to make Jesus known in the unique relational circles that God has given to them.

The Oxford English Dictionary defines the word "evangelism" in a very clear and understandable way, it is "the spreading of the Christian gospel by public preaching or personal witness". It is the second part of this definition that we will be focusing on in this book. My heart behind this book is that you would be empowered to be the best personal witness of Jesus that you could possibly be to everyone in your world! I hope that by reading this, you will be equipped and released to be the soul-winner that God has also called you to be. Through these pages we will take time to carefully unpack what we have known as the Great Commission, making it a very natural and active part of your everyday life. We will explore the motivation (driving force) behind our evangelism as well as discover some incredible, God-given tools that will cause us to be more effective soul-winners. Let us begin by asking some very practical, but honest, questions concerning evangelism as we have known it.

> For us to change the world, as the Lord desires us to, we need to dare to upset the status quo of what we currently believe effective evangelism looks like.

MEETING-CENTRED OR LIFESTYLE EVANGELISM?

For us to change the world, as the Lord desires us to, we need to dare to upset the status quo of what we currently believe effective evangelism looks like. For many years the Church has believed that effective evangelism predominantly happens on a stage. As a result, we have put most of our energy into getting unsaved people to come to meetings, arenas, and evangelistic events. Because of this, we have had unspoken rules and methods regarding what we believe effective evangelism looks like. These methods have encouraged us to persuade people to attend a meeting where they can hear the good news about Jesus, in the hopes that when an opportunity is given at the end of the meeting to respond, they will pray a short prayer and lift their hand to demonstrate what they just did – job done! While these evangelistic meetings should certainly have their place in every church calendar, if this is our ultimate plan for telling the whole earth about Jesus, it is really not working that well. Meetings and one-off events alone are not going to cause the same number of salvations that a more biblical model of evangelism could. To put it even more bluntly, if our current model of evangelism is our ultimate plan for changing the world, then why is it not changing the world? We must re-evaluate the methods of evangelism that we have used in times gone by, and begin to look at how we can reach the whole world, in this age!

IS STREET PREACHING STILL EFFECTIVE?

So, while we are here, let's begin to ask some further questions about present day evangelism. We need to have some honest conversations about the methods that we are currently using and begin to talk openly about the evangelistic methods that actually work and those that no longer work. Let's dare to open up these conversations so that we can be more effective soul-winners.

Being deliberately provocative, an example of one of these questions could be: is street preaching still effective today, or do the people we are trying to reach simply ignore us and walk past? It is honest questions like this one that are going to cause more people to be saved and direct our energies into the most effective methods. Now, I am certainly not against street ministry – when it is done well. I have been involved in a lot of effective street ministry outreaches over the course of my life. In the right circumstances it can be an effective tool for evangelism, but can we also be honest and admit that we have all seen some terrible examples of street preaching. Though we can certainly honour the courage and boldness of the person doing it, sometimes their presentation of the gospel is perceived as nothing more than judgemental, exclusive, and sometimes just downright scary. Street ministry done in the wrong way can push people further away from God, rather than drawing them closer in. I have walked past some street preachers in our city centre and have avoided them, and I am a Christian! I need to confess that I, a pastor, have gone into one store and out of another just to avoid their judgemental accusations and unloving rants. Think about it, if this is how Christians react to street preaching, then how do non-believers react? Yes, I certainly agree that

> Is street preaching still effective today, or do the people we are trying to reach simply ignore it and walk past?

seeds may have been sown by street preachers, but what I am asking is whether or not this is the most effective way for us to be obedient to the Great Commission in our generation.

A common argument for the effectiveness of street preaching is that it worked well in former times. Many people look to Wesley for an example of its power; however, we are no longer in the days of Wesley! Wesley found a way to make Jesus known in his day that produced incredible results; we need to dare to find an effective way to make Jesus known in our day!

I remember watching a street preacher once, who was certainly courageous, and he also had a fairly good understanding of the gospel. Yet, for some reason, he could not see that absolutely no one was stopping to listen to him. With great gusto he continued as people walked on by. Meanwhile, I noticed on the benches not far away from him, there were many people sitting, maybe resting or waiting for their family who were in the shops. I couldn't help but wonder how much more fruit this street preacher would have had from his day if he and his team changed their strategy? What if they turned off the microphone and spent the morning sitting next to people on benches, initiating natural conversations with them about their day, about life, and about God? I understand it would be less dramatic, and you would not have anything to show on your Facebook page of your labours, but the real question is: would it be more effective? If we quantify our success in

> Wesley found a way to make Jesus known in his day that produced incredible results; we need to dare to find an effective way to make Jesus known in our day!

evangelism by the amount of response and engagement in our message, rather than just the number of people who heard our voice, which method would actually be more effective in our generation? It's an open question.

From my experience, people in this progressive culture appreciate honest and intriguing conversations more than being preached at. In my experience, they respond in a greater and more authentic way to a relational approach than to a non-relational one. Again, please allow me to underline one more time that I am not against good-quality street ministry or evangelistic outreaches that get the Church active and on the streets, I just don't believe that this is where evangelism should end, or that we should place all of our hope in this alone to reach our world like the Lord has commissioned us to.

> From my experience, people in this progressive culture appreciate honest and intriguing conversations more than being preached at.

Since the meetings and certain evangelistic methods that we have used are not proving to be as effective in our generation as they did in others, maybe it is time for us to add something else to these strategies? Perhaps we need to consider another model of evangelism? As mentioned earlier, there is a biblical model for evangelism. This model is not new, rather it is truer to the evangelism that we read about in the New Testament, especially in the book of Acts. I am referring to lifestyle evangelism. Lifestyle evangelism does not just encourage the Church to bring others to church meetings, it also mobilises and equips people in the Church to be effective soul-winners in their own day-to-day lives.

This model does not rely on a celebrity preacher or a one-off event, rather it relies on an everyday person who loves Jesus. Allow me to emphasise the point that this is not some newly discovered or radical model of evangelism; rather, it is simply a return to the original design of evangelism. The blueprint plan of God was always for evangelism to be a part of the lifestyle of every believer rather than merely being an event or one-off corporate initiative.

> Lifestyle evangelism does not just encourage the Church to bring others to church meetings, it also mobilises and equips people in the Church to be effective soul-winners in their own day-to-day lives.

So, what about the question: should we have meeting-centred evangelism or lifestyle evangelism? My response is – can we not have both? If the projects we are using are working and result in people finding Christ in a genuine way, then we should certainly continue doing them. But, if they are not producing these results then we must not be hesitant or afraid to rethink, reshape, or even remove them.

My main thought on this subject is simply this: what if we could create a radical paradigm shift in the thinking of the western Church regarding evangelism? A shift towards every follower of Jesus taking personal responsibility for evangelism. By doing this, we would mobilise a sleeping army that could invade the world with the life-transforming message of the gospel, having a greater effect than any of us have ever seen up to now. This change in strategy would also deliver pastors and ministers from being showmen on Sundays, who people come to see. Instead, they could be the "equippers of saints" that they have been called to be. You see, the Church was never meant to be a people storage unit where we are comfortably seated week-in and week-out, to be entertained. Rather, the Church is called to be a place where the people of God are trained, mobilised, and released into the harvest field.

> The Church was never meant to be a people storage unit where we are comfortably seated week-in and week-out, to be entertained. Rather, the Church is called to be a place where the people of God are trained, mobilised, and released into the harvest field.

Today we find ourselves at a very crucial moment in history. Here and now, evangelism is something that we must get right if we want to see the world saved on the scale that Jesus desires it to be. It is time to flow with the Holy Spirit and to see a new level of spiritually empowered ministry. But this time, rather than seeing it only on a stage, we will see it in the lives of believers. How do we begin to see lifestyle evangelism naturally happening in the lives of believers? We will see it by empowering and mobilising the Church to be the Church outside of the walls of the buildings that we so often have been guilty of hiding within. The Church was never meant to be a building, a service, or a weekly meeting, but a community of people called out of darkness into the kingdom of light; a people filled with God's Spirit, who carry the mandate of seeing the world introduced to a personal relationship with Jesus.

We must bring this conversation about evangelism into the lifestyles of believers everywhere. The gifts of the Holy

Spirit are available for us, to empower us, not only on a stage but also on Monday mornings when we wake up to our very normal everyday lives. By enabling the Church to embrace this truth and to have a hunger for the reality of it, we will cause the swing that is needed in our modern culture to make a significant difference. The gospel was never meant to be a sedative that caused a believer to enjoy a restful life; rather the gospel is a stimulant that should awaken believers to a missional life. A life where the commission to see other people encounter Jesus is their personal responsibility.

REDEFINING OFFICES OF MINISTRY

> *And He Himself gave some to be apostles, some prophets, some evangelists, and some pastors and teachers, for the equipping of the saints for the work of ministry, for the edifying of the body of Christ, till we all come to the unity of the faith and of the knowledge of the Son of God, to a perfect man, to the measure of the stature of the fullness of Christ. (Ephesians 4:11-13)*

These verses in Ephesians 4 reveal to us that there are certain offices of ministry that God has called some individuals to; these offices are also commonly known as the ascension gifts. These are gifts that God gave to the Church after Jesus ascended. God still appoints certain people to the office of the apostle, prophet, evangelist, pastor, and teacher. It is crucial that we understand that the purpose of the office, or grace, that these individuals have been given, is not for them to parade around on stages with their ministry title. Instead, the grace is given to them to train and equip others to go, to prophesy, to reach the lost, to take care of people, and to teach the Word. In God's mind, it was never about stages or stage ministry; it was about the equipping of the saints. It was modern Christianity that made the office all about the stage, because in biblical Christianity the office and anointing that accompanied it were always supposed to be about equipping and mobilising. By rewiring our thinking back to a biblical understanding, we are delivering ministry from being trapped on a stage into being viral in the lives of God's people. Then, our Sunday mornings and other gatherings can return to their true purpose of being places of training for the saints (you and me) for what He wants to do next in our communities and circles of influence in the weeks ahead. This means that on Sunday we can simply gather and celebrate what the Lord has done outside the walls of the building during the week, through our lives, rather than just sit there and wait for Him to do it once more on the stage. This would mean that our meetings were no longer the centre of our week, like many of our services have been reduced to.

For our understanding of the various offices of ministry to be complete, we must understand that their purpose is for the training of the saints for the work of the ministry.

> In God's mind, it was never about stages or stage ministry; it was about the equipping of the saints. It was modern Christianity that made the office all about the stage, because in biblical Christianity the office and anointing that accompanied it were always supposed to be about equipping and mobilising.

For example, if we consider the office of the prophet and the gift of prophecy. All believers need to be trained how to correctly prophesy and how to flow prophetically, meaning that they are able to hear and be led by the Holy Spirit in their daily lives. But this does not mean that they are in the office, or ascension gift of a prophet. However, it does give them use of something that God always intended them to have activated in their daily lives. In 1 Corinthians 14, Paul says to the Church (not just to church leadership) that we should all desire spiritual gifts, especially that we would prophesy! So, those who have been given the office of a prophet must be training everyone else to prophesy, as an active part of the role that God gave them. The training and equipping of the saints is also included in the purpose of the office, not just putting the title "Prophet" or "Apostle" on their business card.

> The training and equipping of the saints is also included in the purpose of the office, not just putting the title "Prophet" or "Apostle" on their business card

This way of thinking is true of all the offices of ministry, but our focus in this book is specifically about the evangelist. It is time for us to recognise that the greatest purpose of the call of an "evangelist" is to train others to win souls! They are no longer to just be the one on the stage who is doing it all for others to watch, but they are also to be actively training and releasing others to be effective soul-winners in their daily lives too. The true cure for the western world is an army of God's people who are awake, mobilised, and sent out with evangelistic lifestyles! Nothing less than that will get the job done.

Even though certain offices or ministry gifts have been given by God to certain people, the fruit of each ministry gift should be seen in the lives of the people who are trained and equipped underneath these individuals with an office. This is "the equipping of the saints" that we see in Ephesians 4. It is time for a rewiring of the way that we think of ministry so that we can return to a biblical model of thought, rather than the model we have seen in our culture which has bred far too many spiritual celebrities. With this rewiring, we can then see the equipping of the saints effectively activated in the local church. Just imagine the impact we could have on the world if a large percentage of people who attend our weekly services made the decision to no longer just sit, watch, and be entertained on a Sunday, but rather to be empowered and trained to see God use them daily. Imagine the people who would be impacted beyond the walls of our churches and schedules if people saw themselves as the ministers of reconciliation and ambassadors that the Bible says they actually are!

> The true cure for the western world is an army of God's people who are awake, mobilised, and sent out with evangelistic lifestyles! Nothing less than that will get the job done.

All this is from God, who reconciled us to himself through Christ and gave us [that's every believer] the ministry of reconciliation: that God was reconciling the world to himself in Christ, not counting people's sins against them. And he has committed to us the

> *message of reconciliation. We are therefore Christ's*
> *ambassadors, as though God were making his appeal*
> *through us. We implore you on Christ's behalf: be*
> *reconciled to God. (2 Corinthians 5:18-20 NIV)*

My revolutionary cry is simply this: I see a world that desperately needs to be reached, yet at the same time, an army belonging to God that is fast asleep. It's time for a Holy Spirit inspired awakening that will mobilise the Church again back into the harvest field. It is time to give the Church back to Jesus and the power back to the people! I believe we are standing on the edge of a fresh move of the Holy Spirit, a new era of what He is doing on the earth! But this next move will be very different from ones that have preceded it over the last few decades. It will be all about the empowerment of the seated saints that will cause them to arise and change the worlds they live in. It will be an awakening that makes us uncomfortable again for the gospel's sake. Let's face it, believers have been made far too comfortable for far too long and it is time for another great awakening. This awakening is coming! Are you ready?

Are you tired of just watching ministers on stages show you what they have learned how to do? Is there a hunger in you to get your sleeves rolled up and to see the people in your world come to Christ because of your individual witness? Are you ready for a personal rewiring of what evangelism is and should be? Are you ready to be commissioned and sent out to meet Jesus in the harvest field? Then read on, because you are exactly who I wrote this book for!

THE FIELDS ARE STILL RIPE

Whenever Jesus speaks about harvest, He is speaking about people. He is speaking about people who are currently lost becoming found; people who don't yet know Him as Lord and Saviour finding Him personally and experiencing the new life that comes with knowing Him. Let's look at two statements that Jesus makes about the harvest, that seem identical but actually carry two different messages. Both messages are vitally important when it comes to saving those who are currently separated from a relationship with God. Here is the first statement:

> *Do you not say, "There are still four months and then comes the harvest"? Behold, I say to you, lift up your eyes and look at the fields, for they are already white for harvest! (John 4:35)*

Here we see Jesus imploring His disciples, and also us many centuries later, to not procrastinate in being harvesters. He said, "Don't say sometime in the future, the harvest needs you now!" May that statement echo deep into our hearts today, just as it did when He first said it. May we be motivated to move beyond our excuses to go into the harvest field, hungry to see a generation saved just as the first followers of Jesus were. Keeping this statement in mind, let us now look at the account in the Gospel of

> He said, "Don't say sometime in the future, the harvest needs you now!" May that statement echo deep into our hearts today, just as it did when He first said it

Matthew that initially seems to be similar:

> *But when He saw the multitudes, He was moved*
> *with compassion for them, because they were weary*
> *and scattered, like sheep having no shepherd.*
> *Then He said to His disciples, "The harvest truly*
> *is plentiful, but the labourers are few. Therefore*
> *pray to the Lord of the harvest to send out labourers*
> *into His harvest." (Matthew 9:36-38)*

In these verses we can see that Jesus has the same passion for the harvest as in the first statement. Although, in this account there is a different instruction than in the former. Where He previously dealt with procrastination, this time He underlines two different points:

- The labourers are few;
- Pray to the Lord for labourers to be sent (thrust) into the harvest field.

We have to stop and be honest with ourselves about this first point: the labourers are few. Things today are certainly the same as they were when this was said, being that the harvest is still ripe. But we must also consider the number of labourers who are now available compared to when He originally said it! You see, when Jesus first said this statement, the labourers really were few in quantity. The gospel was a new message; the announcement of a

> With 2.2 billion Christians in the world, we really can't claim that it is due to a lack of labourers that the harvest is not being gathered, can we?

new kingdom on earth, whose King was Jesus – it was radical!
The Church was not yet born because Jesus had not yet gone
to the cross. So, when He said that the labourers were few
– it was very true. His troops were low in number compared
to the amount of people who needed to hear about Him
and His kingdom. But can we really, hand on heart, say that
the labourers are few today? When checking on Google at
the time of writing this book, it
says that there are an estimated
2.2 billion Christians in the world
who are living among a population
of around 7.7 billion people.
With 2.2 billion Christians in the
world, we really can't claim that it
is due to a lack of labourers that
the harvest is not being gathered,
can we? No, I believe if Jesus were
to make that statement today, it
would be very different. More
brutally honest concerning the
excuses and distractions we have
all hidden behind for too long. I
think it would sound something more like the fields are ripe
unto harvest, but the labourers are distracted, apathetic,
self-absorbed, self-obsessed, comfortable, and they don't really
care that people are going to a lost eternity when they die.
They are pre-occupied by less important things and far too
fearful and self-conscious. He could certainly say a number
of things that would be very true – but not that we are few
in number. Let's not be offended by this, rather let's be
challenged to come out from behind the rocks and excuses

> The fields are ripe unto
> harvest, but the labourers
> are distracted, apathetic,
> self-absorbed, self-
> obsessed, comfortable, and
> they don't really care that
> people are going to a lost
> eternity when they die.

that we have been hiding behind; rocks of distraction, fear, and apathy. Instead, let's look honestly at the harvest and with hearts stirred afresh by His love for lost people, let's respond as Isaiah did when He encountered God's heart for the lost and simply say, "Here I am, Lord, send me."

> Also I heard the voice of the Lord, saying: "Whom shall I send, and who will go for Us? Then I said, "Here am I! Send me." (Isaiah 6:8)

Next, Jesus says, "Pray to the Lord of the harvest to send out labourers into the harvest field." Prayer is a vital part of our evangelism lifestyle and it is never wrong to pray and ask the Lord to send labourers into the fields, except if we are excluding ourselves from the prayer! That is to pray, "Lord, send others into the harvest field – but I'm not going!" This would be wrong. We must understand that when we pray for the Lord to send labourers, we include our own lives – not just sending others to do the job for us. Our prayers must include, "Send me, use me, Lord!"

> Prayer is a vital part of our evangelism lifestyle and it is never wrong to pray and ask the Lord to send labourers into the fields, except if we are excluding ourselves from the prayer.

It is similar to when churches have prayer meetings about getting people saved but don't ever mobilise their people to evangelism. The plan is crippled, it is incomplete! It's certainly necessary to pray for the lost to find Jesus but there must also be a commitment in all of God's people to go out and bring them in, otherwise these prayer meetings are nothing more than just nice words and good intentions.

All are called by God into the harvest field and all should have the desire to go! If people say to me that they want to feel closer to Jesus, I tell them to take a step into the harvest field, there you will find yourself standing right next to Him! He is in the harvest field already, beckoning us to come and join with Him in the saving of souls. Naturally speaking, if you want to draw closer to someone you would join them in what they are doing. The same applies to knowing Jesus better. Join Him in seeing the lost saved because that is what He is busy doing.

> If people say to me that they want to feel closer to Jesus, I tell them to take a step into the harvest field, there you will find yourself standing right next to Him!

I pray that this chapter has stirred your heart for the harvest! That you would see it is not the responsibility of your pastors, church leaders, or evangelists – but it is your responsibility also. As we continue unpacking lifestyle evangelism, we are going to look at how we can all be the soul-winners He has called us to be. Remember, all of us are responsible for this harvest that is ripe, ready, and waiting for us!

> *"At the end of the day, the biggest obstacle to evangelism is Christians who don't share the gospel."*
>
> *Albert Mohler*

CHAPTER 2

The Great Commission Made Easy

And He said to them, "Go into all the world and preach the gospel to every creature. He who believes and is baptised will be saved; but he who does not believe will be condemned. (Mark 16:15-16)

And Jesus came and spoke to them, saying, "All authority has been given to Me in heaven and on earth. Go therefore and make disciples of all the nations, baptising them in the name of the Father and of the Son and of the Holy Spirit, teaching them to observe all things that I have commanded you; and lo, I am with you always, even to the end of the age." Amen. (Matthew 28:18-20)

Here we see two different accounts of the charge that Jesus gave to His first followers. This command was to be known from then on as the Great Commission. This was not just a commission for His original followers but, as a result of their obedience, it would become a commission for all future followers of Jesus – including us! Today, in the twenty-first century, we still have a responsibility for this Great Commission. Our King, Jesus, still expects each of us to take the Great Commission seriously, not treating it like it was merely a Great Suggestion! Sadly, some churches even go a step further and treat it like the Great Omission! They are living their Christianity out as if God's call to win the lost was no longer in the Bible. James Hudson Taylor, the great missionary to China, put it so well when he said, "The Great Commission is not an option to be considered; it is a command to be obeyed." The fact that you are choosing to read a book called *Soul Winner*, on lifestyle evangelism, demonstrates that this is not the case for you. I pray that as you read the words of the Great Commission once again, there will be a desire stirring within you to get actively involved with it. As you step forward to take responsibility for it in your own world, you will see heaven's ability offering you everything you need to be the soul-winner He has commissioned you to be; a fruitful soul-winner in the world He has given you to influence for Him.

But let's also be honest that when we first read the Great Commission, especially if we read it in an older translation like the King James, it can appear very daunting. If you are new to the faith and have a heart to be active in evangelism, you could be left thinking, "Wow, that is indeed a huge commission. You want me to go into all the world and preach the gospel to every creature? Okay, but where does

> Our King, Jesus, still expects each of us to take the Great Commission seriously, not treating it like it was merely a great suggestion!

someone like me even get started with that?" The answer to that is simple. First, we need to make it less scary by breaking it down. For example, if you were to feed a young child breakfast, and you gave them a whole cereal bar, then they would probably struggle because of the size of it. That's why cereal companies have cleverly developed smaller versions, like mini shredded wheats, that are in bite-sized chunks. The bite-sized chunks contain everything that the large cereal bars do, but in a more manageable size. That is exactly what we are going to do with this great big commission we have been given. By doing this you will be able to understand exactly what it is that the Lord is asking you to do and also how it is manageable for you. So, let's look at our first bite-sized chunk.

BITE ONE: GO INTO ALL THE WORLD

The first part of the Great Commission commands us to "Go into all the world". So, where exactly should we get started with that? We simply start by getting the heart and the passion to first go into our personal, God-given worlds. When you read this opening statement, you could automatically begin to think of places farther afield – for me, in the UK, that would be Africa, Asia, or remote parts of Europe. If you're like me then you could begin to wonder how someone like yourself is going to go somewhere like that and get people who you don't even know saved. Don't get me wrong, I am an advocate for missions to other parts of the world. I encourage every believer

> Going into all the world starts with first going into YOUR world.

41

to go on short-term trips and I believe that many are called to longer-term mission opportunities. However – it must start with where you are! Going into all the world starts with first going into YOUR world. Before setting sail to the ends of the earth for Jesus, He wants you to feel a sense of responsibility and ownership for your local world. He has already positioned you carefully in a world of relationships that is very unique to you, so that you could have the opportunity to reach that world (your world) for Him!

When we speak about going into all the world, what do you currently see? You might see the world made up of all of the different nations, or perhaps you see the planet earth. Yes, this is indeed "the world" in one context. There is certainly a physical world that we all share and live on. But each one of us also represents an individual "world" too. Think about it, each of us represents a sphere of influence with a circle of people in it that is very bespoke to us. This world includes your family and friends, your neighbours, the people who you work with, the people at your gym, or perhaps people that you meet at the school gates as you collect your kids from school. Think about your world for a moment and the people who are in it. Right now, you have an individual world that is unique to you. It is that world that Jesus wants you to go into first, representing Him and sharing His good news. We could also refer to this local world as your "Jerusalem". This title will make more sense when we read another well-known Great Commission centred verse from the book of Acts. In this verse, once again we see Jesus charging His first batch of followers:

"And you shall be witnesses to Me in

Jerusalem, and in all Judea and Samaria,
and to the end of the earth." (Acts 1:8)

We will be studying this verse in much more detail in our next chapter. But right now, I want you to notice the ripple effect of the different spheres of influence that Jesus called His followers to, paying close attention to which one comes first. First comes Jerusalem! Does that mean that God wants you to jump on a plane and go to the physical city of Jerusalem, in the nation of Israel, to respond to this Great Commission? Or, perhaps is there a larger and more personal meaning for us who are not from Jerusalem? Indeed, there is. When I read this verse, I think of it as God saying to each of us, wherever we may be located in the world, to first take responsibility for seeing people saved and transformed in your unique, local world. That desire to reach people who are further afield is not wrong, it is an admirable desire! We should desire for God to use our lives wherever we find ourselves, and at any time, but He starts by telling us to reach the world we are currently in, our Jerusalems.

After calling people to have an effect on their Jerusalem (the place where they are), Jesus then called us to our "Judea and Samaria". If we continue on the line of thought we have been using, then the "Judea and Samaria" that He is speaking about actually represents the people and places that are slightly beyond the area we live in. Maybe, He is calling us to be active with what God is doing in the cities that we are located, or the nations we live in. The further afield "Judea and Samaria" could also mean sharing Jesus with people who are not a part of our normal relationship circles. Perhaps this is the person at the bus stop, or the stranger in the store. I believe that we can have an impact in our Judea and Samaria by praying, giving, and going. However, this must always be happening alongside the impact we are having in our local world, not instead of reaching our local world.

Finally, He calls us to reach the "ends of the earth", which is self-explanatory. That's what makes this commission so great – it has no end to it. Worldwide salvation is God's desire. He wants to use you and me in all three of the mentioned spheres above. But let me underline once more that worldwide salvation starts in your Jerusalem; the world He has given you, that is bespoke to you!

> Worldwide salvation is God's desire

EXERCISE

So, let's put this into practice. Here is a practical exercise that we can do to help us recognise the people who are in our local mission field, or our "Jerusalem". On the circle provided, write the names of people who are a part of your daily life, who don't yet know Jesus as a saviour and friend.

For example:

- Family members
- Friends (old and new)
- Co-workers
- Classmates
- Neighbours
- People from the gym and community groups

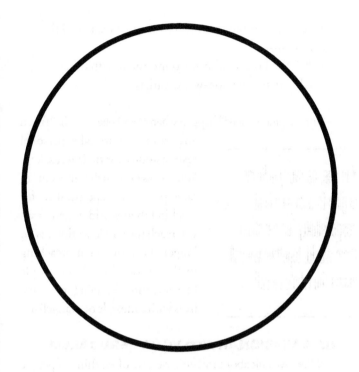

Inside this circle is your Jerusalem! There will be other people who the Lord will bring across your path on a daily basis that you can also include, but it starts here. These people are your personal mission field! You can copy these names and place this list in your office, in your Bible, or on the fridge, and begin to pray them into God's kingdom. Here is a simple plan for how you can now begin to pray for your Jerusalem:

- Pray for them each day, calling them out by name and claiming their salvation.
- Ask the Lord for opportunities to talk with them about what you believe.

- Ask the Lord for moments where you can lead them to Christ.
- Ask the Lord to also surround them with other Christians (the non-weird variety).

Just imagine what will happen when every believer is challenged and equipped to take personal responsibility for their Jerusalem. You see, as every believer begins to take personal responsibility for reaching their world, together we will reach the whole world! It is no longer about one man preaching to the masses, but about people like you and me, living missional lives with a lifestyle of evangelism.

> You see, as every believer begins to take personal responsibility for reaching their world, together we will reach the whole world!

BE A MISSIONARY TO YOUR JERUSALEM

When we talk about missionaries, we often think of people who have gone to preach the gospel somewhere in the outermost parts of the world. Though the title "missionary" certainly describes this type of person, it should also describe you and me. This is not just their title, but it is God's purpose for us, in our daily lives. A missionary is simply someone who is sent with the good news of Jesus to those who have not yet heard it. They show His love to other people in practical and spiritual ways. No matter where we are in the world, near or far, this calling remains the same for us all. Wherever you wake up each morning you need to see yourself as a missionary who is sent by God to where you currently are. You are in your mission field right now

– not just when you get on a plane and go on a mission trip. If it helps, why not put a sign up above the front door of your house that says, "You are now entering your mission field". Then, when you leave the house each day you will remember that you are on mission!

In some ways it can be harder to be a missionary in your Jerusalem than being a missionary to the ends of the earth. What do I mean by that? Simply, that it can often take a lot more integrity and grit to live a life that honours God in front of people who know you than in front of strangers that don't! As I have already made clear, I believe that everyone should go on short-term mission trips and experience evangelism in unfamiliar cultures. Short-term missionaries (e.g. a two- or three-week trip) can be a real blessing to the people they travel to. Not only that, but the experience of a new culture can teach the missionaries a lot and give them a greater perspective and worldview. However, the danger with short-term mission trips is that when you or I get off the plane, we could pretend to be whoever we want because no one knows us. If you wanted to, you could spend the whole time pretending to be someone you are not. Many times, I go on ministry trips and get off the plane to meet a whole bunch of people who don't know me and have no idea who I actually am. I could get off the plane and pretend to be Elvis, Tom Jones, or Tina Turner, and they might never know that I am only impersonating someone else. But if I tried doing that

> it can often take a lot more integrity and grit to live a life that honours God in front of people who know you than in front of strangers that don't!

in the workplace, in my Jerusalem on a Monday morning, then it wouldn't be as well received and would probably get a very different response from those who know me. When you are in your world, where everybody knows you, you have to live out your faith every minute of the day. There's no jumping back on a plane and taking off the wig or costume; you have to walk the walk, not just talk the talk. That takes some real grit!

Please know that I am not saying people who are on the mission field in foreign countries are phonies; I fully appreciate how tough the conditions on the mission field can be, both naturally and spiritually. The point I am making is simply that in far-away places we have the potential to act very differently than we normally would. We could act in ways that we might not ever act around people who really know us and do life with us. So, it can sometimes take more courage and be harder, in some ways, to be a missionary and to live full-on for Jesus in your Jerusalem. The living conditions might be easier, the food will probably not be poisonous, and there may not be snakes or spiders to bite you when you are asleep – but there is the daily challenge of living true to the things you say, in front of those who are constantly watching you.

Something else that we must consider about foreign missions is that when people go to a developing country, it's amazing how they are suddenly able to see the poverty and desperation of the people there. It could almost be like they flick a switch while they are on the plane and suddenly, they are able to see people's needs and suffering. This is not wrong; it is actually a fantastic thing! However, the problem is that some of these people then turn off the switch again on the way home. So that when they arrive back to their normal, everyday, mundane life, they can no longer see the pain and desperation of the people who surround them.

The truth is that if it is behind straw doors or double-glazed doors; whether it be on dusty roads or concrete ones, people with needs and suffering are always there. They could be very different needs, but needs are always present to those who are looking. Of course, the greatest need, wherever you are, is always a person's need for a relationship with Jesus. The ramifications of this need will follow them into life beyond this one. So, let's not be holiday missionaries who experience a romanticised missional way of living once a year for two weeks. Rather, let us be missional people who are ready to be used by God and share His message. Let's meet people's needs wherever we may be, both near and far.

HOUSEHOLD SALVATION

We have looked at the three spheres Jesus said that we should take responsibility for: Jerusalem, Judea and Samaria, and the ends of the earth. But have we missed anyone? Does it really begin with our friends, neighbours, and work colleagues, or is there a group of people that we are overlooking? I am of course speaking about our own families; the salvation of our households.

For some people, you may have already considered your family as a part of your Jerusalem. However, others might have overlooked this as their starting point, and have started focusing on the salvation of friends and colleagues. So, I wanted to add this small section as a gentle reminder to ensure that no one gets missed out. Household salvation is a very biblical thing; God believes in it and so should we!

I have heard it said by numerous people over the years, "If I concentrate on winning other people's family members, then the Lord will send people to save mine." To be honest, I can partially agree with this statement, but not if the person saying it does not feel that they have a responsibility towards the salvation of their own kin. I think the true balance is that we consistently do the very best that we can to make Jesus known to our families by what we say and how we live, and then we also trust God to surround them with other believers who can also enforce the message we have been sharing with them.

> *One of the two who heard John speak, and followed Him, was Andrew, Simon Peter's brother. He first found his own brother Simon, and said to him, "We have found the Messiah" (which is translated, the Christ). And he brought him to Jesus. (John 1:40-42)*

Notice the very first thing that Andrew did, he went looking for his brother so that he could also encounter Jesus. This should also be the attitude of our hearts for our family members, that we don't look over them to see who needs to meet Jesus. Rather, we do everything we can do to lead each and every one of them to the Lord, just as Andrew did. Parents, grandparents, siblings, uncles, aunties, and cousins – let's make sure they are on our prayer list and our lifestyle evangelism "radar", as well as the other people in our Jerusalem.

> When it comes to salvation, God thinks "household"

When it comes to salvation, God thinks "household". Remember when God had Noah build an ark? He instructed Noah to build it for the salvation of him and his household (Genesis 7:1). Similarly, the salvation that He has made available for us, from what is coming at His return, is for us and for our households. So, we need to do everything we can to get them on the ark (in Christ) before the door closes and it is too late!

It's simply about daring to think differently, so that we can realise that when we consider ourselves, we often think in a singular sense, but when God thinks of us, He considers our households too. Remember what Peter said to the jailer after his supernatural release in Acts 16:31, when the jailer asked what he must do to be saved, Peter responded, "Believe on the Lord Jesus Christ, and you will be saved, you and your household." Another way that I think about this is to understand that when God called Andy, He actually called Elmes. He called me and everyone in my name and my bloodline. His desire was that my household and I would be saved, which is true for you also. In the Old Testament we can clearly see time and time again that God's plans and promises were to a person and the generations that followed them. God is still thinking about us generationally. He wants to interact with us in a way that affects those who are called by our name also. As you read through the Old Testament, you will see this principle over and over again (Exodus 20:6, Deuteronomy 7:9, Psalms 103:17). Families and households meant something to Him then and they still do today. So, may we all pray and boldly declare, as Joshua did, "As for me and my household, we will serve the Lord" (Joshua 24:15 NIV).

If you have family members who do not yet know Jesus, then add them to your "Jerusalem" circle right now. Begin to pray for them, asking the Lord for opportunities to share with them, knowing that it is His will that they would experience His salvation too. It's then that you can also ask Him to surround them with other believers; that's the kind of prayer that God would love to answer! Never, ever stop praying and reaching out to them, always believing for them to be saved!

Never forget that lifestyle evangelism is always about more than just the words we speak; it is also about the lives we live. When it comes to religion, the world has met enough hypocrites and experienced enough hypocrisy to last them a lifetime. Our lives must be different! They must be lives that release a better fragrance than that; lives lived for all to see, that match the things we say instead of contradicting them. I have heard it said that a person may not ever read a Bible if you give them one, but they will read your life as they watch you daily live it out. You see, people are actually desperate to see a group of people who live the things they say that they believe. Too often they have experienced people who live contrary to the truths they claim. May that not be us; may we see ourselves as God's ambassadors and live lives of authenticity.

My prayer is that the way people see us live would be louder than the words we speak. May our responses to pressure and the situations that life throws at us, as well as the way we

> Never forget that lifestyle evangelism is always about more than just the words we speak; it is also about the lives we live

love and the way we forgive, cause us to stand out to others and only back-up the things we say. May we know, with great soberness, that evangelism is not just about us speaking, but about living out daily the transformed, new creation lives we claim to have.

A SUCCESSFUL SOUL-WINNER'S FIRST JOURNEY

After looking at how we can reach the whole world, by going to our Jerusalem, then Judea and Samaria, and onto the ends of the earth – let's also look at the first journey every successful soul-winner must take. On this journey towards missional living, the first journey we must be willing to take is to live beyond the boundaries of ourselves. Daring to live beyond our own, self-made boundaries will enable us to be successful soul-winners everywhere we go, whether it be near or far. To live beyond yourself means to no longer be restrained by the boundary lines that you once had. I am talking about simple things like our comforts, preferences, and conveniences. To reach a dying world effectively, a soul-winner needs to take a trip beyond these carnally inspired needs so that they are able to be used by God wherever and whenever He needs them, regardless of convenience. This is a part of the "dying to self" that the Bible often refers to (Galatians 2:20; Luke 9:23).

It's amazing how often we can be guilty of letting our

> On this journey towards missional living, the first journey we must be willing to take is to live beyond the boundaries of ourselves.

comforts and preferences have too much of a voice in our lives. We all need to bring these things into submission to God and submission to His plans. Let me give you a simple real-life example of this to make it clear. I can remember at the close of a service one Sunday morning, a man was waiting for me, obviously wanting to speak with me. It had been a good Sunday all-round, with ten people responding to the salvation call at the end. Not knowing what this man would say, I approached him to ask. History had taught me that normally by doing this it would lead to either an encouragement, or a criticism about the service we just had. Either of these things I am always willing to hear, especially if the person has a good spirit. So, I asked this gentleman how I could help him, and his response came immediately; it was: "I liked three of the songs you used today in worship but not the third one." My initial reaction to the man, knowing that he was a Christian and had been saved for many years, was to remind him that worship was not for him to enjoy, but it was for God. I went on to explain to him that perhaps there was a possibility that when we were building Church that day, seeking God for the right word, and selecting worship songs that we felt would be right to connect people to God, that just maybe we were not thinking about him. Perhaps we were thinking also about the ten people who responded to Jesus at the end. Maybe by reaching the ten unsaved, we actually got it right – if this is one of the ways we quantify success of services we hold.

I could see this came as a bit of a shock to the man – dare I say, it was even revolutionary – but I think he got the point. The point was that the service was not built around his preferences. We all have the potential to have a bit of this in us, don't we? We know the songs we prefer to sing, the things we want the pastor to speak about, and how we like to spend time after the service; these are the things we need to be able to lay down so that God can do what He needs to do, even if it's not in a way that we prefer. A blunter way of putting it is that we need to get over ourselves if we want to win others!

Effective soul-winners will purpose in their hearts that they will live beyond their preferences for the cause of Christ. If living beyond what is a preference to us, or what we feel makes us comfortable with something, causes lost souls to be saved then that is the place we should choose to live!

There is always a price that needs to be paid to see a person saved; sometimes it includes laying down our preferences, other times it is giving our time to a person when we don't have much time to give. It could also mean giving our money to go somewhere to reach someone, which could look like buying them a meal, or purchasing an air ticket to get to them. There are so many examples of things we need to be willing to give away to reach others, but until we journey to a place that is called "living beyond ourselves", then we are not going to be willing to pay the bill for lives to be saved. Considering this, let us not forget Jesus, who modelled so clearly for us that you have to be willing to give your life away to save the world that you have been sent to. Throughout the pages of the gospels, Jesus constantly gave His time, attention,

> Effective soul-winners will purpose in their hearts that they will live beyond their preferences for the cause of Christ

and love to every single person He encountered, whether they were a city official, a prostitute, or a leper. He constantly gave and gave of himself to benefit the lives of others. For all the good He did to others, what was His thanks? To be hung on a tree, not thanked, but mocked. In His final words, He still gave himself away, as He prayed, "Father forgive them, they don't know what they do."

> **let us not forget Jesus, who modelled so clearly for us that you have to be willing to give your life away to save the world that you have been sent to**

Soul-winner, if you want to change the world, then be willing to pay whatever price you need to. Take that first mission trip, to go beyond the preferences, comforts, and rights that you once defended. If you do this then you will find that you are an instrument in the hand of God, that He can use whenever He needs to.

> *"If you live by the same values and priorities [Jesus] had, you will find evangelism happening naturally. It becomes a life-style and not a project."*
>
> *Rebecca Pippert*

BITE TWO: PREACH THE GOSPEL TO EVERY CREATURE

You might read the second part of the Great Commission, "preach the gospel to every creature", and respond: "But I am not a preacher", or perhaps, "I can't see myself preaching to anyone, let alone to every creature". So, let's switch-up the wording a little to make it more doable. First, what does it mean to preach? To preach means simply to communicate, and all of us can communicate, especially when it comes to personal, one-on-one evangelism where we are dealing with individuals rather than large crowds. You see, everyone in the world is preaching, both saved and unsaved alike. Everyone is passionately talking about something or someone they love. Maybe it's a football team, a car, or a hobby. Like I said, the world is full of people preaching about the value and love they have for certain things or people, and that is all we are doing when we tell someone about Jesus. We are using our words, as well as living out our lives, to communicate to people how incredible Jesus is to us; how wonderfully He has changed our lives, and how He can change theirs too.

What if we remove the word "preach" for a moment, from the Great Commission, and replace it with a word like communicate, tell, chat, or discuss? How much less intimidating is this commission now? You see, this is the truth: Jesus simply wants you to go and tell others about Him in a way that is true to who you are and how you would naturally communicate on a day-to-day basis.

When you have a relationship with God, and not just a religion about Him, it is easy and natural for you to include Him in conversations. Your relationship with Jesus should be the very thing that fuels an embarrassment-free introduction of Him to others, where you desire to present Him in a way that they will want to know Him too. It can be a natural thing!

I have been married to my wife Gina for over twenty-six years, and we have five wonderful kids. Whenever I am talking with people, it is never too long before Gina or the children appear in that conversation, often with accompanying photos. I do not have to force them into the conversation because my love for them always gives a very natural entrance into it. I don't sit there in conversations with people struggling, feeling obliged, or wondering how am I going to mention Gina, or how am I going to let them know how proud I am of my kids. Never! It happens naturally because of who they are to me and the love that I have for them. In the same way, who Jesus is to us and our knowledge of what He has done for us should be what fuels us speaking about Him to others in a very natural and everyday way.

I remember talking to a youth group once and my message was called: Stop Treating Jesus Like an Ugly Girlfriend. In my message, I compared a young man's relationship with a new girlfriend to a person's relationship with Jesus. I painted this scenario for them: imagine if you spent a night out with your new girlfriend and the whole night you told her how beautiful she was and how much you adored her. Then, on the way home, you turned a corner and saw a bunch of your friends from school. Instantly, without thinking twice, you shoved her into a nearby bush. When your friends asked, "Didn't we see you with someone?" you adamantly denied it, convincing them they were seeing things. But as soon as they left, you reached into the bush and pulled the young lady out, apologising and putting your actions down to some strange nervous reaction you have.

You could be lucky enough to get away with that once, but if you did that again then I would like to think she would come to the conclusion that you were embarrassed of her; recognising that you act one way in private and another in public. I explained to the youth how this is what we are like when we don't let people know that we love Jesus, or don't tell them who He really is in our lives. Let's face it, this is not just a message for young people, is it? The fact is that when we do this, we are denying Him. Even though it's because of fear about what they might think of us – we are still denying the one who should never be denied. Here's a real sobering verse on this thought:

> *Therefore whoever confesses Me before men, him I will*
> *also confess before My Father who is in heaven. But*
> *whoever denies Me before men, him I will also deny*
> *before My Father who is in heaven. (Matthew 10:32-33)*

The good news is that God does not want you to get yourself a wooden box and stand on it to preach to your friends; He is just asking you to be ready to communicate the truth about who He is and what He has done for you. He simply wants you to bear witness to what you have experienced so far in your relationship with Him. When someone is a witness, it is because they were present when something happened. Therefore, if we have a relationship with God, then we have witnessed Him for ourselves. It is from this personal experience that we are able to introduce others to Him in an authentic

> The good news is that God does not want you to get yourself a wooden box and stand on it to preach to your friends; He is just asking you to be ready to communicate the truth about who He is and what He has done for you.

way. He is not asking you to preach at them violently, or to hit them with deep theology and random facts from the Bible that they don't need to know. He simply wants you to bear witness to who He is in your life, how He has saved you, and how He wants to do the same for them.

> He simply wants you to bear witness to who He is in your life, how He has saved you, and how He wants to do the same for them.

In Psalms 107 it says, "Let the redeemed of the Lord say so, whom He has redeemed from the hand of the enemy." I can vividly remember singing this in church growing up, it was a catchy little tune, but I have never understood it like I understand it now. It's a simple instruction for those who have been redeemed by God to not hold back from "saying so" to others. It is a call to let other people know how He has so wonderfully and so completely redeemed us (purchased us back) to himself. This catchy little psalm makes even more sense when you read it in other translations.

So, go ahead – let everyone know it! Tell the world how he broke through and delivered you from the power of darkness and has gathered us together from all over the world. He has set us free to be his very own! (TPT)

Let the redeemed of the Lord tell their story – those he redeemed from the hand of the foe, those he gathered from the lands, from east and west, from north and south. (NIV)

Go ahead and tell everyone; let the redeemed tell their story. Each and every one of us has a powerful story of redemption. It tells of how He restored a lost relationship between us and Himself, and how He restores our lives daily. No two redemption stories are exactly the same; they are individual, like the people they belong to, but they all point to the same redeemer. So, go ahead and start telling everyone your story because it's your story to tell![1]

USE YOUR TESTIMONY

Our story, or personal testimony, is such a powerful thing because it tells people about what we have personally experienced for ourselves. Other religions and cults don't have these testimonies because they only have religious teachings or deceptive thought patterns that have been inherited from others, but you are different, you have a personal relationship with your God. Unlike the Jehovah's Witnesses, who knock on your door and can only tell you what they have been taught, you can testify about what He has personally done for you and what He is still doing. It is so key for anyone who wants to be an effective soul-winner to know their testimony and to be able to share it at any chance they get.

Your personal testimony should include things like:

- What your life was like before you encountered Him.
- How you encountered Him, both the moment and the journey to that moment.
- What happened when you received Him and His salvation, and how you felt.

---

1 Read Andy's book *iamredemption* (Great Big Life Publishing, 2014) to learn more, and to read other people's stories of redemption. Visit greatbiglife.co.uk to order.

- What happened immediately after you received Him as Saviour and what changed in your life.
- What He has done for you since as you have walked with Him.
- How He has blessed you, healed you, or given you breakthroughs.
- How your life is different because of Jesus.

These are just a few examples of things you can include, there are of course many more. Another beneficial thing to do, if you have not done so before, is to take some time to write your testimony down, maybe including some of the things listed above. This enables you to be able to see the natural sequence of your testimony, and to then put it in a layout that is easy to remember so that when you get a chance to share it, it flows in an easy and precise way. I was taught by a mentor to be able to share my testimony in five minutes. This has been a useful tool for when time was limited, and I did not have the luxury of having longer to share with someone. Why not try to write down your testimony so that you are able to share it with others?

So, we can now change the previously scary, "Go ye into all the world and preach the gospel to every creature", to a very doable, "From now on, step into your bespoke world every day with a passion to communicate the truth of Jesus and what He has done in your life in a way that is unique to you." That's much easier, right?

WHAT FUELS US TO BE WITNESSES?
The "why" behind the "what" is always very important, isn't it? Among other things, it is the motivator behind

what we do and the passion that we do it with. So, why should we tell others about Jesus and the salvation that He offers? What should fuel us to want to tell those in our local worlds about Him? Religious obligations are not enough. Though we should feel a sense of obligation after discovering the pure love of Father God sending Jesus to die for us, this is not the "why" that should drive us to a lifestyle of evangelism.

Being obedient to the command given to us by Jesus is again a valid motivation but even more so our motivation should simply be our love for Him; a love for Him and a love for what He loves! God loves people and still longs that none would perish (2 Peter 3:9). This love for people is what fills His heart, so as His heart daily becomes our heart then His love for people who are currently separated from Him should naturally become ours too.

I once heard it said by a group of Christians in a place that I was ministering that all that matters for a Christian is their personal proximity to God. They went on to say that all we are called to do is sit on Papa's lap, even adding to this that evangelism was just dead works, all that mattered was our closeness to Him. To be honest I found this way of thinking to be quite warped, somewhat disturbing and only partially true at its very best. You see, yes, we are certainly called to close proximity with Him and to sit on His lap, as a child upon a loving father. But the reality is that if you get that close to Father God and find yourself with your head on His chest then you are inevitably going to hear His heartbeat, right? What's the heartbeat of God? Souls, souls, souls! That none would perish but all would find the new creation life He paid for them to have!

You see, God loves all people, excluding none, and longs for them to know Him and to experience the salvation (wholeness) that He offers. As people who have been redeemed and restored, we are now ambassadors of His heartbeat to all men. Remember that in God there is no racism, segregation or any other man-made thing that causes His offer to be for just some or a certain group. Rather, it is a message of salvation and new life to "whosoever believes" (John 3:16). Let us read the verses from 2 Corinthians again, that speak of the ambassador's heart we are to carry and the plea we should all naturally have because of our knowledge of what He did for us:

> if we say we love someone then why would we not tell them about the one who can save their soul from a lost eternity and give them a life worth living?

> *Now all things are of God, who has reconciled us to Himself through Jesus Christ, and has given us the ministry of reconciliation, that is, that God was in Christ reconciling the world to Himself, not imputing their trespasses to them, and has committed to us the word of reconciliation. Now then, we are ambassadors for Christ, as though God were pleading through us: we implore you on Christ's behalf, be reconciled to God. For He made Him who knew no sin to be sin for us, that we might become the righteousness of God in Him. (2 Corinthians 5:18-21)*

To think about it in an even more blunt way: if we say we love someone then why would we not tell them about the one who can save their soul from a lost eternity and give them a life worth living? Isn't that selfish? Even if it is because of very real things like the fear of man, how could we justify keeping this incredible truth from people? Is this not to be like a man who finds a goldmine that holds enough gold for himself and anyone else who needs it, yet after finding it he takes what he needs and then hides the entrance so others can't benefit from it also?

Dear reader, heaven and hell are real and so is a lost eternity for all those whose names are not in the Lamb's book of life. It's not a fairy tale and we need to stop treating it like one. Rather, we need to allow the Holy Spirit to blow the fairy dust off our understanding of heaven and hell so that our hearts are mobilised to see everyone one day arrive in the right place, especially those who we say we love. We can't save anyone, only Jesus can do that. But we can carry and clearly communicate the message about the one who can save; bringing it to every person, especially those who we would consider close to us. Let your love for them override any fear you have about encountering a negative response.

Always remember that your choice to be obedient to the great commission does not save you in any way because He has already saved you. Neither can it add to your salvation because that also is completed in Him. Your obedience to obey this commission is certainly

> **Let your love for them override any fear you have about encountering a negative response**

a demonstration of your love for Him but it never adds to or takes away from His love for you. That love has already been demonstrated, completed and sealed through all He has done in and through Jesus. It is vital that we keep a healthy understanding of this, otherwise we can find ourselves drifting into the arena of dead works. That is where we think that by doing certain things it will make Him love us more, or in some way, save us more than we already are saved. This is not true because nothing we do can add anything to a perfect, finished salvation (Hebrews 2:3). What drives us to go must be an obedience that is fuelled by love and gratitude, and nothing else.

> **What drives us to go must be an obedience that is fuelled by love, gratefulness and nothing else**

SO, WHAT SHOULD MOTIVATE US?

- The knowledge of His great love for us, what He has done for us and also what He desires to do for others.
- Our love for Him and what He loves.
- Our desire to walk in obedience to Him and His Word (His command).
- The privilege of being invited by Him to be an ambassador and co-labourer with Him.
- A pure love for people and a desire for them to experience Him like we have.
- A sober understanding of the reality that heaven and hell are real.
- The knowledge of the choice between an eternity with Him or an eternal separation from Him for those who don't receive His salvation while they are alive.

"Oh, my brothers and sisters in Christ, if sinners will be damned, at least let them leap to hell over our bodies; and if they will perish, let them perish with our arms about their knees, imploring them to stay, and not madly to destroy themselves. If hell must be filled, at least let it be filled in the teeth of our exertions, and let not one go unwarned and unprayed for."

Charles Spurgeon

CHAPTER 3

Empowered to be Witnesses

But you shall receive power when the Holy Spirit has come upon you; and you shall be witnesses to Me in Jerusalem, and in all Judea and Samaria, and to the end of the earth. (Acts 1:8)

Here is some more really good news: the Lord is not expecting you to do this in your own ability or strength! A key part of His Great Commission has always been to provide the power and the ability for you to be the witness He is calling you to be, by placing His Spirit in you. When reading about the promise of the Holy Spirit's coming in the book of Acts, it is vital that we see that the primary purpose of the Holy Spirit coming into a person's life is to empower them to be witnesses. The word used for power here is the same root word used for dynamite! It is an explosive ability, not a mere candle-light flicker. Others have translated this word to mean ability, meaning that we receive divine ability (His ability) to do what He is asking us to do when the Holy Spirit comes upon us. Others say it also means force, that the force of heaven is released in and through our daily lives to accomplish on earth what He asks us to do. Either of these definitions is good, or you can enjoy all three.

> *But you shall receive power when the Holy Spirit has come upon you; and you shall be witnesses to Me.*

Sadly, many well-meaning, Spirit-filled believers have made the coming of the Holy Spirit all about the sensations they can experience, like goosebumps in meetings, instead of grasping the primary purpose. Not that the Holy Spirit does not give us sensations but let us agree with scripture concerning His coming which is firstly about the empowerment of witnesses. When you better understand the context of the moment that Jesus was in when He made this promise and who He made it to, it makes a lot more sense.

Allow me to paint the picture. Jesus had come to earth and proclaimed His kingdom. He had raised up some faithful followers and deposited His kingdom in their hearts. He had died and was now risen from the dead and about to ascend to be seated at the right-hand side of the Father in heaven. He then left the mission of saving the whole world in the hands of these faithful followers and the cities and regions they had been called to were filled with people who were violently opposed to them and the message they carried. Many of these oppositions were from religious leaders who believed that the message of Jesus violated everything they believed about God and His plans for the people of Israel. The lives of these early believers were in great danger and they were under daily threat of imprisonment and death because of their allegiance to Jesus and His message of the kingdom. Though these men had been with Jesus when He walked the earth, they still had very real fears and apprehensions within about their own ability to take the message they had been entrusted with, not only into the different areas of Israel, but also to the ends of the earth.

This is why, before ascending, Jesus wanted to assure them (and us) that they would not be doing it merely in their own strength but that the Holy Spirit was coming to empower them to be the witnesses that He had called them to be. That the Holy Spirit in them would successfully fulfil the task of reaching the world that Jesus had committed to them as they yielded their lives to Him. When you look at the verses that precede the one we have opened this chapter with, you can see a group of people who were getting ready to do it in their own strength. Then, Jesus comes and stops them, saying "Not yet, wait". Why, after calling them to go, was He now asking them to wait? Because they were not yet ready! They had not yet been filled with His life and clothed with His divine ability.

> And being assembled together with them, He
> commanded them not to depart from Jerusalem, but
> to wait for the Promise of the Father, "which," He
> said, "you have heard from Me; for John truly baptised
> with water, but you shall be baptised with the Holy
> Spirit not many days from now. (Acts 1:4-5)

The reality was that, though they had been saved by Jesus' death and resurrection, they were still the same ability wise as they had been before. They were still living by their own natural strengths and abilities and not from that which would be provided by the one who was coming soon – the Holy Spirit!

The next stop on our Pentecostal journey is obviously the upper room, where we see the coming of what the prophets had foretold, what the Father had promised, and Jesus had told them to wait for – the glorious coming of the Holy Spirit.

> *When the Day of Pentecost had fully come, they were all with one accord in one place. And suddenly there came a sound from heaven, as of a rushing mighty wind, and it filled the whole house where they were sitting. Then there appeared to them divided tongues, as of fire, and one sat upon each of them. And they were all filled with the Holy Spirit and began to speak with other tongues, as the Spirit gave them utterance. (Acts 2:1-4)*

Notice that firstly the Holy Spirit came and filled the whole house where they were sitting. Their best description of this moment was to say that it was like fire filling the room. But then they saw this cloud of fire break off into unique individual flames, with a singular flame coming upon the life of each person there. In that moment every person in the room was personally filled with God's Holy Spirit with one initial evidence being that they started speaking in a heavenly language they had never learned.

It is important for us to separate the corporate (crowd) experience and individual experience of the filling of the Spirit in these verses so that we can fully grasp the truth of what God was doing in this divine moment of church history. When His Church was born in fire.

You see, the coming of the Spirit was not for a corporate experience alone, but for the divine empowerment of every person present. He was given to personally enable each of them to know the leading of the Spirit, the teaching of the Spirit, and also the empowerment of the Spirit to bear witness of Him, as they had been commissioned to do earlier. When teaching on the coming of, and the baptism in the Holy Spirit, it is vital that we base what happened upon what the prophets foretold (Joel 2:28, Ezekiel 36:26, Matthew 3:11) and what Jesus clearly taught us would happen (John 14:16-17, 15:26, 16:7, 20:22 and Luke 11:13). Also, it is vital for us to establish that there is no verse in the Bible that instructs us that the Holy Spirit was ever recalled back to heaven! Why? Because His assignment was not yet completed. Which means that He is still present here today and is filling the lives of believers and empowering them to be the witnesses God needs them to be in our generation.

Sadly, there are some people today who have not experienced this promise of a baptism in the Holy Spirit. This is most often because of ignorance, which is the sad result of some people not letting others know about the availability of this glorious gift. Scripture clearly reveals that the gifts of God and the baptisms we are to receive in our walk with Him are two-fold. There are two gifts and baptisms available to every believer, not just one. When it comes to the two baptisms, we understand that one of these baptisms is the baptism in water, which is relative to our repentance, redemption and regeneration in becoming a new creation. The other is a baptism of Spirit, which is done by Jesus. This baptism empowers the believer to be able to live out the new life they have received through placing their faith in Christ.

John the Baptist recognised this and so should we:

> *I indeed baptise you with water unto repentance, but*
> *He who is coming after me is mightier than I, whose*
> *sandals I am not worthy to carry. He will baptise you*
> *with the Holy Spirit and fire. (Matthew 3:11)*

Jesus recognised the ministry of John to baptise people in water gladly submitting to it Himself to fulfil all righteousness (to do what was right) but notice how John also recognised the baptism of the Holy Spirit and fire that would come through Jesus to every believer who asked.

> *Then Jesus came from Galilee to John at the Jordan to*
> *be baptised by him. And John tried to prevent Him,*
> *saying, "I need to be baptised by You, and are You*
> *coming to me?" But Jesus answered and said to him,*
> *"Permit it to be so now, for thus it is fitting for us to*
> *fulfil all righteousness." Then he allowed Him. When*
> *He had been baptised, Jesus came up immediately from*
> *the water; and behold, the heavens were opened to*
> *Him, and He saw the Spirit of God descending like a*
> *dove and alighting upon Him. (Matthew 3:13-16)*

To live the victorious overcoming life that Christ Jesus died for them to know it is vital that a believer both hears about and receives both of the gifts that God has made available for them. Sadly, some never hear of the second gift, so they live lives exempt of the empowerment that is available to them. This was the case for a man who Paul met in Ephesus called Apollos.

> *And it happened, while Apollos was at Corinth, that*
> *Paul, having passed through the upper regions, came*
> *to Ephesus. And finding some disciples he said to them,*
> *"Did you receive the Holy Spirit when you believed?"*
> *So they said to him, "We have not so much as heard*
> *whether there is a Holy Spirit." And he said to them,*
> *"Into what then were you baptised?" So they said, "Into*
> *John's baptism." Then Paul said, "John indeed baptised*
> *with a baptism of repentance, saying to the people that*
> *they should believe on Him who would come after him,*
> *that is, on Christ Jesus." When they heard this, they*
> *were baptised in the name of the Lord Jesus. And when*
> *Paul had laid hands on them, the Holy Spirit came*
> *upon them, and they spoke with tongues and prophesied.*
> *Now the men were about twelve in all. (Acts 19:1-7)*

The great news is that this second gift, the baptism in the Holy Spirit, is available today just as it was for those who were in the upper room and for those men who we read of in the above verses. His gift of salvation through Jesus was not selective or for just a few handpicked followers and neither is the gift of the Holy Spirit; it is for all who desire it.

So how does a person receive this second gift? The same way you received the first gift. What did you do to receive salvation? You heard about it, asked for it and received it by faith, without any need of evidence or feelings, right? You know that it became yours from an inner witness and then you simply began to live in the good of it. Receiving the second gift of God is exactly the same, being based on the Father's faithfulness to His Word and ability to do what He promised; not on your ability to receive in any special or laboured way. Simply thank Him that His Word declares that the baptism of the Holy Spirit is available for you and that you would like it, then thank Him for it and receive it, as with everything you get from God by faith.

As we stated at the start of this chapter, it is this baptism of the Holy Spirit that enables us to be the witnesses we are truly capable of being. Yes, we can attempt to do it in our own strength but the real issue for me is: why would we, when such a glorious better option is freely available to us all? The difference in your witness will be supernaturally different because you will have received a supernatural upgrade.

> it is this baptism of the Holy Spirit that enables us to be the witnesses we are truly capable of being

Let me grab one of the men that were in the upper room to use as a case study, so you can see the difference that this supernatural upgrade can make in your life as a witness for Jesus. Let's do a before-and-after analogy looking at Peter as a witness before the empowerment of the Holy Spirit and then after it. In the closing chapters of the gospels we see Peter, who, though he had made many grand statements promising that he would never deny Jesus, in one moment deny Jesus three times. When people asked Him "were you not His follower too?" Peter's response was to violently separate himself from ever being associated with Jesus, only to hear the cockerel crow out three times, just as Jesus had foretold that it would. On a side note, isn't it wonderful that Jesus knew Peter would fail Him and yet He never stopped loving him or removed the plans that He had for him?

A little later on we witness the great comeback plan that Jesus had for Peter, on a seashore after His resurrection. But at this moment in the storyline we see Peter, defeated, crushed and disillusioned, having denied Jesus before just three people. When it came down to it, that was the sum total of his own ability – a minus three. But then we read of the upper room and the day of Pentecost, and we read of how the Holy Spirit filled the lives of all within it, including Peter. The very next thing we see is a man called Peter preaching boldly to thousands of people and, as a result, three thousand of them respond to his very blunt, unashamed, unapologetic gospel message. Wait a moment – was this the same Peter who denied Jesus before? Yes, it was! But he was now changed, he had become empowered with God's own Spirit and it was that empowerment of the Spirit that had taken him from -3 to +3000 in one moment.

> You see, you were never expected to do it in your own strength, just as the first disciples were not expected to do it in theirs

It is the same for us today, it is God's Spirit now in us that enables us to be the witnesses and fruitful soul-winners that He has commissioned us to be. You see, you were never expected to do it in your own strength, just as the first disciples were not expected to do it in theirs. No, you receive power when the Holy Spirit comes upon you and then you become witnesses for Him in your Jerusalem, further afield and even to the ends of the earth.

> God is not looking for us to provide the ability, He is looking for us to provide our availability.

God is not looking for us to provide the ability, He is looking for us to provide our availability. Like it is said so well in Zechariah 4:6, that it is "'Not by might nor by power, but by My Spirit,' says the Lord of hosts." The question then is two-fold: are you available for the Lord to use you to reach others and have you been empowered by His Spirit to do so?

FIRST COMES YOUR GO; THEN COMES HIS POWER

As a good friend of mine once said: "What is it about the word Go that the church does not get? Is it the G or the O?" It's not a big word, is it? Sometimes our lack of drive to go as we are commanded can be about different fears that we may have! Yet, as we have seen, the Lord has now provided His power and ability to the person who will obey the call and go.

One blockage could be that common issue that we can all struggle with sometimes, called "feelings over faith"! So many people today, in the modern Church, always want to feel something before they will do anything. Whether it be worshipping, serving or giving, many Christians today won't do the things they are meant to, or only do them sometimes, because they are not "feeling it". Your feelings should never be the determining factor of what you do for God and His kingdom; being led by His Spirit and His Word are what we should go by. God is not asking you how you feel about it! He wants you to walk in obedience to what He has asked you to do, when you feel like it and when you don't! This is also true when it comes to our response to the great commission because He has instructed us to go and so when we do go, we will always experience the ability He has provided.

A sad thing that I have seen today is that people are sitting in churches waiting to feel the power, or the ability, to go before they will go. However, God never works like that! As with everything about Him, we are to walk by faith and not by sight, or any other feeling, because He is a God who always responds to faith. First, we step out in faith, believing what He says He has given, it is then that we experience the reality of it in our situation. Allow me to labour this point again: too much of the modern Church today is led by its feelings and only do the things they are meant to do when

> As with everything about Him, we are to walk by faith and not by sight, or any other feeling, because He is a God who always responds to faith.

their feelings give them permission to do so. When these things should be a lifestyle to us. This is nothing more than carnal Christianity, a walk with God that is subject to your feelings. The reality is that you will never experience the miracles and other big things that God wants you to if you remain imprisoned in this wrong way of thinking. We are called to be a people of faith, who walk by faith in all that we do. What does this look like with our commitment to personal evangelism? We go simply because He told us to and we go expecting to experience His ability because He said He would provide it. How we feel about it should not even be a matter we give any serious consideration to.

His power is in position for us, but it can't flow until we go! Like an electric kettle or a power drill that is plugged into the wall, everything is in place to make a hot drink or to drill through the wall, but nothing actually happens until you press the button, or put a demand on what is available. It's time for the Church to break free from sense-related fears and disobedience and to step out into the harvest field with obedience and faith, trusting His Word that as you do, He will be there with you. As you open your mouth, as He promised the disciples, He will provide the words for you to say.

> We go simply because He told us to and we go expecting to experience His ability because He said He would provide it. How we feel about it should not even be a matter we give any serious consideration to.

> *"Now when they bring you to the synagogues and magistrates and authorities, do not worry about how or what you should answer, or what you should say. For the Holy Spirit will teach you in that very hour what you ought to say." (Luke 12:11-12)*

So, go ahead and put a demand on the Holy Spirit, who is now living within you. Step out and begin to share your faith more than ever before and I guarantee you will feel an adrenaline-like empowerment to do so as you do. You will hear wisdom and answers coming into your mind and out of your mouth that you know did not come from you. It is one of the best feelings you can ever experience, the feeling of God using your life to communicate His love and plans to another.

POWER EVANGELISM

When it comes to what the Lord has given us to be effective harvesters and to get the job done, it just keeps on getting better! Not only has He given us His Spirit and made our lives His temple and dwelling place, but the Bible reveals that the Holy Spirit has brought His toolbox with Him to enable us to have all that we need and more to get the job done correctly. If you call a plumber to come and fix a leak in your house you would be disappointed if they did not arrive with their tools to get the job done, right? Well the Holy Spirit has brought His tools with Him for us to use; they are called the gifts of the Spirit. They are not like everyday hand tools; these are power tools! Let's have a look at these tools that are available for us to use whenever we need them. As we do, let me underline again that I believe these tools were never provided just to show off in church services but rather to use on the harvest field to get the job done!

There are diversities of gifts, but the same Spirit. There are differences of ministries, but the same Lord. And there are diversities of activities, but it is the same God who works all in all. But the manifestation of the Spirit is given to each one for the profit of all: for to one is given the word of wisdom through the Spirit, to another the word of knowledge through the same Spirit, to another faith by the same Spirit, to another gifts of healings by the same Spirit, to another the working of miracles, to another prophecy, to another discerning of

> *spirits, to another different kinds of tongues, to another*
> *the interpretation of tongues. But one and the same*
> *Spirit works all these things, distributing to each one*
> *individually as He wills. (1 Corinthians 12:4-11)*

We see from these verses that the Spirit makes these gifts available for the profit of others and He distributes them as He sees fit or needed. Those who have been around the Church for a while might need to again break some old mind-sets they picked up along the way in order to experience the realities of what is now available to them. In many churches it was taught that certain individuals in the Church got certain gifts and you went to those individuals if you needed to experience the benefits of that gift. This meant that the gifts of the Spirit were "owned" by the certain few, whereas the truth is that the gifts belong to the Spirit and the Spirit of God makes them available to whoever needs them, whenever they are needed.

Other people have argued over what the best gift is. Well, that can be answered simply. The best gift is the one you need for the task at hand. Again, using a plumber as an example, if the job he is working on needs a wrench, then a saw isn't beneficial for the task at hand. The plumber needs to be able to reach into his toolbox and pull out the tool that he needs for the job he is doing. Though a very simple analogy, this is how it works for us when we desire to use the gifts of the Spirit to minister to others.

For example, if you need to see physical healing for a

> The best gift is the one you need for the task at hand.

person who you are witnessing to, in order to show them that God is real and that He means business, a word of prophecy is not what you need – you need the gift of healing or working of miracles. Another myth we need to remove is that these gifts are only for church leadership! That is not true; the gifts of the Spirit are for every believer to use to minister to others. As Paul said: they should be earnestly desired by all, "Pursue love, and desire spiritual gifts, but especially that you may prophesy" (1 Corinthians 14:1). Paul spoke this to the whole church, not to the church leadership.

As we consider the classic verses we know as the Great Commission, let us not forget the other sending verses in the gospels. Those that record that Jesus sent His disciples out to do the work of the ministry while He was still present with them. Notice what He told them to do, it went way beyond just sharing the good news of the salvation message:

> And as you go, preach, saying, "The kingdom
> of heaven is at hand." Heal the sick, cleanse the
> lepers, raise the dead, cast out demons. Freely you
> have received, freely give. (Matthew 10:7-8)

Let us also hold these verses in context, the disciples were sent to do this before Jesus had risen from the dead and before they had been filled with the Holy Spirit. They were operating in the name and authority of Jesus alone. We have now also been given the name of Jesus and His authority to use but we have also received His Spirit, who is now living in us. How much more should we expect things to happen as we go with His Spirit?

Also notice how these commands given by Jesus go hand

in hand and carry the same intent as the ones He gave when commissioning His people to go in the commission verses of Mark 16.

> *And these signs will accompany those who believe: in my name they will drive out demons; they will speak in new tongues; they will pick up snakes with their hands; and when they drink deadly poison, it will not hurt them at all; they will place their hands on people who are ill, and they will get well." (Mark 16:17-18 NIV)*

Remember, Jesus never told His disciples to stop operating in power; religion did! In fact, He encouraged them to have the faith to do so, even saying they could do what He did, and even more!

> *Most assuredly, I say to you, he who believes in Me, the works that I do he will do also; and greater works than these he will do, because I go to My Father. And whatever you ask in My name, that I will do, that the Father may be glorified in the Son. If you ask anything in My name, I will do it. (John 14:12-14)*

These are incredible verses that show us the heart of the Lord for His representatives on earth who are called to operate in the power of the Holy Spirit. If you continue to read on from this verse, the very next thing that Jesus begins to teach on is the coming of the Holy Spirit to dwell in the life of the believer. It would have been enough for the Lord to say "you will do the things you have seen Me do", but He goes even further and says "greater things will you do"!

To be honest, if my life currently matched what He did then I would be amazed, how about you?

We must be willing to be taught by the great teacher, who now lives within us, how to use these gifts that are available. The reason it has been mainly church leaders who seem to operate in these gifts is that, sadly, it is predominantly the

> Remember, Jesus never told His disciples to stop operating in power; religion did!

church leaders who desire to operate in the gifts. We all must be actively desiring the powerful gifts of the Holy Spirit that are available!

Look at these wonderful gifts of the Spirit that the Father has made available to us. Here they are categorised in what is commonly taught as their three groups:

REVELATION GIFTS
- Word of wisdom
- Word of knowledge
- Discerning of spirits

POWER GIFTS
- Faith
- Gifts of healings
- Working of miracles

INSPIRATION GIFTS
- Prophecy
- Different kinds of tongues
- Interpretation of tongues

For me to do justice to teaching on these gifts and their various applications and expressions in the life of the believer, we would need a whole other book! When you begin to take the time that is needed to unpack each one of these incredible gifts there is so much that can be taught on each of them. But let us remember that the purpose of this book is to challenge and equip you in lifestyle evangelism, so please allow me to remain focused on that purpose and just take this moment to recognise, celebrate and encourage you to desire these gifts. There are many wonderful books available today for you to further study these gifts and I highly encourage you to do so.

Suffice to say that each one of these gifts can be so incredibly effective when witnessing to someone. Whether you reveal something to them that they know you could not have known, or you provide the wisdom of a way forward in a situation that they did not see before. Or maybe you speak prophetically into a situation they are facing, or you pray for them and see healing happen or miracles break out in their lives. It may also be that you discern or have inside knowledge about something they are not telling you. Whichever gift it may be, they all flow from Him to you as He makes them available for you to use to minister effectively to others. Isn't that wonderful? It displays how God has, as He promised, given us the ability to do the things He has sent us to do. He has given us tools to use and they are not just tools but power tools!

The expression of these gifts in our lives should be a natural thing even if they are, of themselves, supernatural things. You don't have to become dramatic when using them or put on a show. Simply let them flow through you in a way that is natural to you for the benefit of the one you are ministering to. It's always about having one ear open to the person you are witnessing to and another ear (your spiritual ear) open to what the Holy Spirit is revealing about them, or the situation they may be in. Stay away from dramatic statements like "Thus says the Lord" or "God told me"; rather, use everyday language that does not violate their personal judgement of whether what you are saying is true. When ministering to people I have just met, I am always careful not to freak them out or cause them to think I am a weirdo, because then they will stop listening to the things I am saying. I often use language like "Hey, I am just getting the impression" or "Forgive me if I am off track with this but I am strongly sensing this". I am still telling them what I believe the Lord wants them to know but in a way that is palatable to them and does not skew their view of God.

Over the years of using the gifts of the Spirit in my evangelism I have spoken to many people about things they experienced in certain grades of school. I have given people the names of their family members that are in crisis and answers to situations they were going through that they thought no one knew about. All of these things and many others have enabled me to give evidence of a real God, who really knows them. The Lord will always do things like this to enable you

> Whenever the Holy Spirit releases a gift for you to use, it is never to glorify yourself; it is always to glorify God.

to get to the point, by catching their attention; this is so you can then reach them for Him! Other times I have prayed for them and seen God heal things in powerful, undeniable ways; this made it really easy to then introduce them to

God, who is the One that just did something impossible for them. Always remember that whenever the Holy Spirit releases a gift for you to use, it is never to glorify yourself; it is always to glorify God. The gift is used to catch their attention in a real way or release something that God has for them. Stay pure of heart with this and the Holy Spirit will use you time and time again to handle His power tools. My encouragement to you is simply to have a go! If you do it in a way that is respectful and non-threatening, then they will very rarely ever be offended. Equally, when you begin to realise the things you are hearing are the thoughts that the Spirit is giving you then faith arises, and you just keep on doing it. So, what if you get it wrong? Are they going to stone you to death for caring? The question is: what happens when you get it right? Lives are changed, healed and restored by the power of God flowing through you!

> The question is: what happens when you get it right? Lives are changed, healed and restored by the power of God flowing through you!

"He is not seeking a powerful people to represent Him. Rather, He looks for all those who are weak, foolish, despised, and written off: and He inhabits them with His own strength."

Graham Cooke

CHAPTER 4

Fishers of Men

*And as He walked by the Sea of Galilee, He saw Simon
and Andrew his brother casting a net into the sea; for they
were fishermen. Then Jesus said to them, "Follow Me, and
I will make you become fishers of men." They immediately
left their nets and followed Him. (Mark 1:16-18)*

Look closely at the offer that Jesus made to these fishermen:
"follow Me and I will make you". When it comes to
lifestyle evangelism and being an effective soul-winner for
Him, He already has a plan to make you everything you
need to be – all you need to do is follow Him with a desire to
learn. Jesus had stopped and seen these brothers fishing and
must have loved the skill they used to bring the nets, filled
with fish, into the boats. Maybe it was as He watched them
catch fish, He saw their potential to catch something of
much greater value? Men! He knew that the skills they had
learned over many years that harvested netfuls of fish would
be perfect skills for harvesting netfuls of souls.

So, Jesus wandered down to the Sea of Galilee, where they

were, and laid out a new job opportunity by simply saying, "Come, follow Me and I will teach you to fish for men." The Bible records that immediately they dropped the nets that had defined them in their past, to follow Him and they picked up a new kind of net that would now define the course of their lives. Leaving their equipment, friends, security and family businesses, they walked away to follow Jesus into the harvest field and be trained by Him to win the hearts of men and women for God. How about you? Will you hear His call to you today to be a fisher of men? Will you follow Him into the harvest field? Are you ready for the Lord to train you to fish for souls? Then believe me when I say that you have His attention!

LEARNING TO FISH

Fishermen can teach us many things about catching souls for Christ. There are many great comparisons that we can learn from them to enhance and improve the strategies we use to reach people. One lesson that immediately stands out to me is the way that fishermen use different lines and different bait to catch different kinds of fish. The bait you use to reach one variety of fish can be radically different to what you need to reach another. Worms might entice some fish while a completely different bait will catch another. Also, the fishing line you use is very important: the line you use for salmon will be very different to the line you use to catch a shark. Are we able to think this way when it comes to reaching people? Or are we too stuck in a limiting "one size fits all" way of thinking?

We need to always be ready and able to adapt our presentation of the gospel to reach different types of people that we meet, but never to water down the message. People are different depending on things such as their age, culture, where they grew up or how educated they may be. The reality is that people can be very different indeed and we need to be able to be like the Apostle Paul and "be all things to all men".

> *Though I am free and belong to no one, I have made myself a slave to everyone, to win as many as possible. To the Jews I became like a Jew, to win the Jews. To those under the law I became like one under the law (though I myself am not under the law), so as to win those under the law. To those not having the law I became like one not having the law (though I am not free from God's law but am under Christ's law), so as to win those not having the law. To the weak I became weak, to win the weak. I have become all things to all people so that by all possible means I might save some. (1 Corinthians 9:19-22 NIV)*

Paul never compromised himself, his standards or what he believed to reach people, but he was always willing to re-invent himself and his approach to people for the purpose of winning them! Notice how it says that he became like those he was trying to reach; this meant he was not afraid to come down to or rise up to their level and to speak the language they spoke. Paul had an incredible chameleon-like ability when it came to winning the lost, he always used wisdom and initiative to reach different types of people in different ways and was a master of using the language of their lives, so that they understood. As he did this he effectively and consistently caught the attention of whatever crowd he found himself with.

He also knew how to apply wisdom to his soul-winning which always enabled him to have a great catch. When it comes to winning souls, wisdom is another very important thing to have. Proverbs 11:30 teaches us that "he who wins souls is wise". If someone does not use wisdom when telling someone the gospel, then they could lose their audience before they even get to the point! If they say or do something unwise then they could easily lose the person they are wanting to reach! The Holy Spirit is the Spirit of wisdom and He is now within us. If we will take the time to listen to Him, He will always give us the wisdom we need to effectively reach people in a way that works. This can be wisdom about when to speak, how to speak and also when to stop speaking! He will also help by reminding you of everyday examples that enable you to communicate God's heart to the hearer in a way that they understand, just as Paul did.

Remember, Jesus always used everyday things to communicate what He wanted people to understand. He never preached over their heads or in a way that normal folk could not grasp. Rather, He always came down to our level and used vines, farmers, pearls, lost coins and so many other everyday things to make the point He wanted to make in a way that the hearer would understand and always remember. If we allow the Holy Spirit, He will teach us to do this when we keep our ear turned towards His wisdom. I remember once being in a very remote part of the Philippines where there was no electricity and the men of the village made their living by fishing the waters outside their huts. The pastor I was with asked me to share about Jesus to these men and women who had never ever heard about Him. As I looked at them and thought about the things I needed them to understand, I asked the Holy Spirit for the best way forward. Instantly it came to me! I began my talk through a translator by saying, "Let me tell you about some fishermen." I proceeded to tell them about how Jesus loved and saved fishermen, all of them fully understood my very simple gospel message and all gladly received Him as Saviour! I had to remember that it was not about letting them know about all the things I knew, but rather it was about communicating clearly what they needed to know to start a relationship with Jesus. We need to be able to get over ourselves and all of our knowledge and always be ready to simplify our message to see people understand and respond to it. It's not about sharing all that you know, it's about sharing what they need to know! I have spoken to many different types of people over the last 30 years and I've been able to see so many become saved because, like Paul, I dared to take the message God has given me and make it understandable to people's unique worlds.

> It's not about sharing all that you know, it's about sharing what they need to know!

Another skill that good fishermen understand is timing. They know when to reel the fish in or bring the net into the boat. They have learned by experience that when they get this wrong, then they lose the catch. We need to have the same wisdom and patience when leading people to the Lord, sometimes we can be in too much of a hurry. Yes, I believe that there are certain people who need to be reeled in quickly, especially if they don't have time to wait, for example a person on their deathbed. We should always be ready when prompted by the Spirit to present the gospel with great urgency and get them in the boat before we leave them. However, there are times when we should be more tactical and apply greater patience. First take time, as a fisherman would, to lay out the bait (causing initial intrigue), then gently, over time, you reel them in.

Just like the fishermen I see when I am walking along the shore of the beach near to where I live, I believe we should always have a number of lines out at once and be faithfully checking them and slowly but surely be reeling them in constantly. What does this look like in your Jerusalem, that place you live day by day? It looks like starting conversations wherever you go: the gas station, restaurant, school gates or workplace. The art of conversation is a very important skill when desiring to win souls. In the next chapter we will look at this further, but let's lay out what this could look like with some very practical steps:

> The art of conversation is a very important skill when desiring to win souls

First, you just simply start up a conversation! That may seem shallow to you, but it is actually providing the doorway for you to take them into the area of conversation you want them to be in. Yep, you're hearing me correctly – the great journey of leading them into a relationship with Jesus most often starts with a simple hello.

Then, over the course of the next few conversations that follow you can begin to speak about church and your belief in God, maybe start by asking them simple questions like what they did at the weekend. They will usually go ahead and tell you what they did and then respond by asking you the key question: how about you? This is the moment you were waiting for, now you can begin to tell them about church and an ongoing topic of conversation can begin.

Suddenly you have rapport with them and can frequently chat about all manner of things, including your faith in God. It is then that you will find they begin to give you permission to share what you believe, and they might share what they believe. This is not a time to preach to them or make them feel judged, simply answer their questions and bear witness to who Jesus is to you.

Now you simply maintain the line you have thrown out, manage that line with integrity and authenticity. Always welcome open conversations where you can agree to differ with certain things, with an agenda to keep away from arguments and stay connected in conversation. Remember your purpose is never to win an argument but to win the person! Always remember that Jesus has not sent you to condemn them or to judge them but to help them to find the salvation and wholeness that is available in Him.

> Remember your purpose is never to win an argument but to win the person!

HE DIDN'T GIVE US THE MINISTRY OF CONDEMNATION BUT OF RECONCILIATION!

Now all things are of God, who has reconciled us to Himself through Jesus Christ, and has given us the ministry of reconciliation, that is, that God was in Christ reconciling the world to Himself, not imputing their trespasses to them, and has committed to us the word of reconciliation. Now then, we are

> *ambassadors for Christ, as though God were pleading*
> *through us: we implore you on Christ's behalf, be*
> *reconciled to God. (2 Corinthians 5:18-20)*

He never came to condemn them so neither should we.
Many people have become experts of John 3:16 but far too
many stop reading too soon and don't get to verse 17 – you
see, Jesus had not finished speaking.

> *For God so loved the world that He gave His only*
> *begotten Son, that whoever believes in Him should not*
> *perish but have everlasting life. For God did not send*
> *His Son into the world to condemn the world, but that*
> *the world through Him might be saved. (John 3:16-17)*

Let me underline again this very important truth: He never
came to condemn, but to reconcile
and save! May we always bear this

He never came to condemn, but to reconcile and save!

in mind when we find ourselves in
moments where it is tempting to
put on the judge's wig; if He didn't
come to condemn then neither
should we. Not that we are to ever compromise what we
believe, or validate wrong beliefs with the people we are
speaking to, but with love and a heart that is not out to
condemn, we should speak the truth in love, respecting the
person we are looking to reach just as Jesus always did.

Over the years I have seen evangelism done well by many
people, but I have also seen it done in very wrong and ugly
ways. The worst I ever saw was while I was ministering to
people on the streets of New Orleans during the infamous

festivities of Mardi Gras. I had gone with a team of young students to be a part of an outreach on the streets during this festival which is basically a celebration of all things sinful. Don't get me wrong, it was a very challenging environment to share about Jesus, as the people were there to enjoy everything that is opposite to the kingdom of God. There was drunkenness, drug addiction, nudity and perversion being demonstrated openly on every street corner. We were there to tell these people about a love that was better, a love that was pure that could transform their lives like none else could. Many churches send outreach teams to the streets over that festival and it was a joy to meet other soul-winners who were there to be light in the darkness and to show the people in confusion the love of God. But there were other groups there who called themselves Christians but were nothing more than religious thugs. They were standing with insulting banners and placards as they screamed through megaphones with violent shouts of how everyone was going to hell and how God was going to kill and harm those who would not listen to them! Not only was their message wrong and repulsive to the hearer, but the spirit they operated in was unloving and condemning, drawing nothing but mockers and a large circle of avoidance. For me the highlight was when they began to scream at me and those who were with me that we were going to hell too because we would not stand with them and judge the people coming past. Meanwhile, all around them were God-loving people having real and honest conversations with the people making their way through the streets. These soul-winners were giving away hugs, bottles of water and time to listen. These mostly unseen, uncelebrated saints reached many broken and confused people by sowing seeds of truth and hope that would remain long after Mardi Gras was over. How do we quantify the success of our evangelism? Is it by how it makes us feel or made us look, or is it by the people who were genuinely affected by the time we spent with them sharing Christ?

When it comes to our lifestyle evangelism may we all be like wise fishermen, constantly throwing our lines into the ocean of lost souls. Believe me, if you learn to do this well you will always get a bite on your line. When you find that someone is open to hear, be careful (Spirit led) with how fast you move forwards. Sometimes, in our zeal, we can lose the people we could have won if we would have applied more wisdom. Remember that what we are offering is a change of life, not a subscription to a magazine! I have seen people evangelising who acted like a man walking into a bar and asking a stranger to marry them before they introduced themselves, they were just too full on! Unless prompted by the Spirit, never be in so much of a hurry that you lose them before you properly introduce them to Jesus. Rather, we should take the time needed to get them saved correctly rather than having them pray a prayer just to shut you up and get rid of you! Remember that he who wins souls is wise.

> We must be aware that we are part of a bigger picture and our part is to sow some seeds into their journey towards Christ.

SOMETIMES YOU ARE A PART OF A PROCESS!

It is useful to bear in mind that there are times when we may not be the ones who win someone to Christ. Rather, we must be aware that we are part of a bigger picture and our part is to sow some seeds into their journey towards Christ. Most often when someone has been won to Christ there has been a longer process to getting to that point and if we are the one to lead them into the kingdom then we were included in that journey. When doing an altar call at church I am very conscious that if people respond to Jesus in that moment it is normally the result of the hard work of many people. When as a pastor I give the opportunity for them to respond to Jesus, I enjoy the privilege of harvesting what is the hard work of so many people who have faithfully sown seeds into that person's life during the journey. Other people before me had witnessed to them, given them their testimonies or challenged them with the good news of the gospel. I just had the wonderful opportunity to be involved at the moment of final harvesting!

The harvesting moment is such a great moment to be a part of, but I need to remain conscious that other times my role in the process of what God is doing in a person's life is just to sow a seed and someone else will bring the harvest in! Always humbly remember that no matter who is doing what, it is always the Lord who is bringing the increase!

I planted, Apollos watered, but God gave the increase. So then neither he who plants is anything, nor he who waters, but God who gives the increase. Now he who plants and he who waters are one, and each one will receive his own reward according to his own labour. For we are God's fellow workers; you are God's field, you are God's building. (1 Corinthians 3:6-9)

Our role is to be ready whenever and wherever we are to communicate to others who Jesus is and what He has done for them. If we get the privilege to pray them into the kingdom, then praise God, but if our part is to sow a seed on their journey to that moment then praise God for that opportunity too.

> *But in your hearts revere Christ as Lord. Always*
> *be prepared to give an answer to everyone who asks*
> *you to give the reason for the hope that you have.*
> *But do this with gentleness and respect, keeping a*
> *clear conscience, so that those who speak maliciously*
> *against your good behaviour in Christ may be*
> *ashamed of their slander. (1 Peter 3:15-16 NIV)*

WHAT'S HAPPENING BENEATH THE WATER?

The final lesson I will draw from fishermen is very simple, yet it is profound for those who want to be effective fishers of men. It's this: a fisherman is always conscious that there is more going on beneath the water than he can see on the surface. He knows that even if he cannot see with his eyes what is happening beneath the water, there are things happening. The only slight exception being a fly fisherman who is using polarised glasses. So how does this relate to us? In two ways: one is very natural and the other is very spiritual. Let's deal with the natural one first.

> A fisherman is always conscious that there is more going on beneath the water than he can see on the surface.

When sharing Jesus with someone, always remember that

you probably don't know what is truly happening in their life. Most people project a lifestyle, an emotion, or a state of being, even if it is not true. They may, to some degree, project an image of what they want you to see or what they think you want to see. Just as a fisherman knows that there is more happening than they can see, we must be aware that their real-life condition might be different from the one they are projecting. In fact, it could be very different from the show they are putting on for you. People can wear all different types of masks in their daily lives, lives that might be similar to a well-rehearsed masquerade. God sees beyond our performances and will give you words that cut through the projection and reach the real life that most would not see. When this is happening, you could feel that what you are sharing with them is not at all relevant, as they are obviously okay in this area, only to later find out it was spot on. Be aware that you might just be seeing the show they are putting on or the life they put on display for people to see, when actually things are broken, hurting, confused and desperately in need of God. Like the account of the Samaritan woman at the well in John 4, they could seem to be holding it all together nicely on the outside while inside there is actually mass confusion. Just as Jesus cut through the performance into the real world of this lady, who was trapped in the guilt of multiple adulterous relationships, He still uses us to do that today! Never ignore the prompting of the Spirit when He is revealing something that looks very different to the picture you are seeing naturally. Beneath the surface of a person's life, they desperately need the life and salvation that Jesus is bringing to them through you.

Let's now look at the second example of when there is

more happening beneath the surface than can be seen, this time looking spiritually. When having a conversation, we need to be sensitive to where someone is spiritually when we are trying to lead them to Christ. Though you may not always see it or be aware of it, an unseen battle is taking place over a person's life. The battle is between God who wants to save them and set them free, and the devil who does not want to let them go. Every person belongs to the devil and he is their spiritual father until the moment they turn to Christ and are born again. It is in their new birth, when they die to the rule, reign, and ownership of the devil, that they are translated into a new kingdom where God is now their heavenly father, the devil having no more claim.

He has rescued us completely from the tyrannical rule
of darkness and has translated us into the kingdom
realm of his beloved Son. (Colossians 1:13 TPT)

Let me put it this way: the former owner, or father, does not want to let the child come out of his abusive grip into the loving arms of a father that will love and restore them. He does not want another empty seat on his coach to hell because someone else got on God's bus, which is heaven bound. The moment you begin to open the door to Jesus, the devil tries to slam it shut as quickly as he can. This battle between good and evil, between Satan and God, is all taking place beneath the waters, where the person involved does not see what is happening. But we must see what is happening beneath the waters! The moment you start leading a person to Jesus, a spiritual battle breaks out over their life that they do not understand and are not equipped to fight.

When soul-winning we must be conscious of what is happening beneath the waves in the person's life and the battle that is now on for their eternal soul. Spiritually, this means we should be praying for them, not just speaking to them. Without sounding "super spiritual", we must understand there is a spiritual battle that is happening, and God is fighting in that unseen place for them, alongside the natural conversation that we are having. The following verse underlines this reality:

> *Finally, my brethren, be strong in the Lord and in*
> *the power of His might. Put on the whole armour of*
> *God, that you may be able to stand against the wiles*
> *of the devil. For we do not wrestle against flesh and*
> *blood, but against principalities, against powers,*
> *against the rulers of the darkness of this age, against*
> *spiritual hosts of wickedness in the heavenly places.*
> *Therefore take up the whole armour of God, that*
> *you may be able to withstand in the evil day, and*
> *having done all, to stand. (Ephesians 6:10-13)*

As the great evangelist, Reinhard Bonnke, put it so very well, don't forget that when you are leading a person to Christ, you are "plundering hell and populating heaven"! Without being weird about it, be conscious that you have positioned them in a spiritual battle that they don't understand, unless they have experienced the spiritual realm before through something like witchcraft. Prayer is a definite key and it is non-negotiable! Pray protection over them from the deception and schemes of the enemy.

In addition to the spiritual considerations, you can also

help them practically. I have seen it so many times when someone is invited to church or to meet up so that they can hear the gospel. When the day comes, they don't come and when you meet them again, they tell you something that happened to them on the way. It normally goes something like this: they were getting ready to come and all of a sudden, their kid threw up on them, the dog fell down the stairs, the microwave blew up and the car would not start. All of these things may seem very natural, especially to them. But actually, most times, that is the devil at work throwing everything he can at them to stop them coming. Why? Because if they come, they will hear the gospel and could respond to it and when they do that then he loses his claim on them. So, I always teach people to be aware of the spiritual battle that you sign people up for when you invite them to church. Let me say again that it is a battle they are not presently equipped to understand or to fight. So, when you invite someone to church or to meet up with you, don't just invite them, take another step and pick them up or meet them beforehand. This little extra step could be the thing that gets them where they need to be to find Jesus. If you are currently an "inviter" that's great, but now graduate to being a bringer too! Do your very best to help people with the spiritual unseen world of what is happening as well as communicating the gospel to them naturally. Like a fisherman does, always think about what is happening beneath the surface, both naturally speaking and spiritually too.

> *"Evangelism is not a professional job for a few trained men but is instead the unrelenting responsibility of every person who belongs to the company of Jesus."*
>
> D. Elton Trueblood

CHAPTER 5

How to Start a Conversation

*When Jesus came into the region of Caesarea Philippi,
He asked His disciples, saying, "Who do men say that I,
the Son of Man, am?" So they said, "Some say John the
Baptist, some Elijah, and others Jeremiah or one of the
prophets." He said to them, "But who do you say that
I am?" Simon Peter answered and said, "You are the
Christ, the Son of the living God." (Matthew 16:13-16)*

When it comes to lifestyle evangelism, in your Jerusalem, purpose to always be including people you don't yet know alongside those you do. Maybe that waitress in the restaurant or the person waiting in line for the bus. The most difficult thing for a lot of people about speaking to others about Jesus is simply this: how do I get started? So, how do you initiate a conversation with someone about Jesus? Like we have established, I honestly believe that the most effective plan for evangelism in our modern world is not street preaching or evangelism outreaches, but rather it is training the people of God to share their faith effectively in their daily lives. Once again, let me say it's not that other models of evangelism are wrong, it is simply that lifestyle evangelism is proving to be more effective and has longer lasting results. One of the reasons it is proving to be more effective in the long term is because when people personally lead others to Christ, they then have the responsibility of getting them planted in a church and are able to be around to disciple them.

The most difficult thing for a lot of people about speaking to others about Jesus is simply this: how do I get started?

When looking at how to train people in lifestyle evangelism, we have to dare to look at the blockages that prevent them from wanting to do it or make them feel that they can't do it. If we are brutally honest, most of these blockages are normally to do with fear or lack of confidence. If we don't take the time to remove these blockages, then we won't see an army of soul-winners released like God desires. There also needs to be an element of practical training for people when it comes to evangelism and soul winning. This training should firstly involve teaching people about the gospel and what they believe so that they can have greater confidence in sharing it. But we also need to help people understand something that is a lot more natural, something that falls within the boundaries of communication skills. We need to teach people how to be effective when communicating their faith, how to be effective communicators. This, as I have said, is a more practical aspect of preaching the gospel, but it is still vitally important. Training in communication skills will help a person's confidence so that they can successfully share what they believe about

God and the salvation He offers.

So, when the rubber hits the road, what is it about communicating our faith with another person that we feel awkward or nervous about? Perhaps it is that we have the heart and the desire to share about, but we don't feel we have the right words to do it. This can be solved by learning how to initiate normal and effective conversations with the people that we come into contact within our daily lives!

When we take the time to break it down even further, then perhaps we are unsure of what is the best question or statement we can use to lead us into a meaningful conversation with another person? What should that question be that could initiate a positive conversation about our faith? Or to put it another way, what's a good opener?

I am actually going to start by looking at some potentially bad opening questions, but to preface that I want to add that we must always be willing to visit the perception of the person we are

> **We need to teach people how to be effective when communicating their faith, how to be effective communicators.**

talking to and to ask ourselves what they might think about the question we are asking them. It might make sense to us, but we need to think: does it make sense to the one we are reaching? What will that question sound like from their perspective? This might sound really simple, but it is always beneficial to think this way so that we avoid saying things that could cause us to be misunderstood or shut our communication down before we get started. For example, I know of people who are trained in evangelism that are taught to ask this initial question: "If you were to die tonight, do you know where you would go?" or "Do you know if you would go to heaven or hell if you died?" Okay, the question is honest and real, but imagine if you had never been near a church or around church folk and someone asked you that question? To me it could sound a bit too much like a threat. Before I was saved, people would speak to me like that when I was in bars, it was normally just moments before fists started flying. Needless to say, that was not the right question to ask me. Though I thoroughly agree there are certain times and places for a question that is as blunt or straightforward as this. For example, when you are around a deathbed, when time is limited and where the question of where this person will spend eternity is unknown. Also, in a moment where you feel the Spirit prompts you to be so direct as to ask this type of question. But let's step away from these scenarios and back into normal, everyday life for a moment. Is there possibly a better question to ask, one that is less threatening and that could cause greater intrigue in the mind of the listener?

> Perhaps we are unsure of what is the best question or statement we can use to lead us into a meaningful conversation with another person?

I personally believe there are better questions to ask, especially if you are looking to initiate a meaningful conversation. Let me tell you about the one specific question that I use a lot, which has proved to be very effective. It actually came from a time when I was pursuing the Lord for the most effective way to start a conversation about Him with another person that I did not yet know. Like you, over many years,

I have heard the suggested questions like "If you die tonight do you know where you will go" and, feeling uncomfortable with them, I prayed, "Lord, those questions do not work for me in most situations, what else can I ask? Almost straight away an answer came to me from Him that was so simple, it was pure genius. An answer that had been there all the time in the Bible, but I had not seen it like I was suddenly seeing it now. What was that answer? I felt the Lord say to me, "Why not ask the question I asked?" Straight away my mind went to the verses we used in the opening section of this chapter that are taken from the moment Jesus asked His disciples, "Who do people say that I am?" They responded by giving Him the commonly used answers that they had all heard others use, "You are Elijah, or a prophet." This was no more than a Google response; it was like they had typed into Google, "Who is Jesus?" But then Jesus asked the same question on a more personal level, "But who do you say I am?" This time the public consensus was silenced, and one man spoke out of personal belief and conviction: "Lord, you are . . ."

> Like you, over many years, I have heard the suggested questions like "If you die tonight do you know where you will go" and, feeling uncomfortable with them, I prayed, "Lord, those questions do not work for me in most situations, what else can I ask?

That right there was the question I was looking for. A perfect question that could initiate a good conversation with a person that did not threaten them but left a wide-open gap for them to respond honestly, thus starting a conversation that was genuine. I was very excited about this discovery, but before telling others to use it I needed to take this opener on the road myself for a test run to see how it worked. To my surprise and delight it worked perfectly! One of the first people I used it on was a waitress at a restaurant in Pennsylvania; as she brought the bill, I thanked her for great service and then said, "Can I ask you a question? And I need you to tell me what you really think, not what you think I want to hear." Very intrigued, she said, "Yeah, sure." I said, "Okay, here we go: who do you think Jesus was?" It went quiet for a moment and then she responded, "Wow, that's a good question." After thinking for a little longer she said, "I am not fully sure, but I know that He died for my sins on a cross." Straight away I knew what level to come in at with her and what direction to go in with my following questions. So next I asked about whether or not she was raised in a Christian home, which she was. Then I asked, "Do you feel that you have a relationship with Jesus outside of the one that your parents have?" From there we entered a very honest and meaningful conversation where I was able to tell her about how a relationship with God is different to a religion about God. At the end she agreed to pray this prayer before she went to sleep that night: "Jesus, if you are real then prove it to me." You know as well as I do that Jesus will always take a deal like that.

Very happy with my first test drive of my new opening question, I got into the habit of asking waiters and waitresses that same question wherever I went. I also found that if you ask it before you pay the bill, or before you put your pin number in the payment machine, then they will give you all the time you need. Sometimes I make it sound like they are helping me with a survey or a paper I am writing, to make it feel even more natural or as though it is a part of the conversation I am having with the other people on my table. Sometimes I ask, "Who do you think He was?" other times "Who do you think He is?" Since doing this I have had so many incredibly different answers to that simple question. I've heard everything from "I believe He is the Son of God" to "He was a nice guy", right the way to Him being a magician, con-man and astronaut. But my point is that each answer led me naturally into a great conversation with the person that sometimes meant I could pray with them. Other times it just challenged their ideas of who Jesus was and the love He has for them.

Many of the times when I have continued to talk to people after asking this question, I have felt the Holy Spirit telling me something about them or giving me a word of wisdom for them, only to see their amazement of how exactly right it was. Many respond by saying, "How would you know that?" The Holy Spirit will often do this if your ears are open to Him, to help you get to the person's heart or to underline that you are hearing God for them. Remember that the plan for their salvation is not something you have come up with; you are partnering with God to see them saved and He will give you everything you need to do so, including the gifts of His Spirit. Sometimes you might find yourself with the privilege of leading them to Jesus in that moment; in other cases, you will be in a position to carry on

> The joy of knowing you were co-labouring with God to see their soul saved and their lives transformed is a feeling second to none.

the conversation at another time. Perhaps your conversation is one of many vital components of the plan God has to eventually win them to Himself. Either way the joy of knowing you were co-labouring with God to see their soul saved and their lives transformed is a feeling second to none.

When you work out a natural way to initiate conversations with people about Jesus it is like a roadblock is removed and there is nothing stopping you anymore. I hope that this simple opening question that I often use has encouraged you; please feel free to use it yourself! I have found it to work very successfully. If you want to try something else then, like I did, ask the Lord to give you one or two "openers" of your own. When He does, send an email to me and share them so I can have a go with them too! Every effort of evangelism is valuable but when you can do it effectively it is powerful. When you manage to connect with a person as you communicate to them about Jesus, something supernatural happens and the Holy Spirit begins to bring them closer and closer to Jesus.

> When you work out a natural way to initiate conversations with people about Jesus it is like a roadblock is removed and there is nothing stopping you anymore.

GOD WILL USE YOUR UNIQUENESS

God has wired you to be unique and He is able to use your uniqueness to reach people that others can't, in ways that others can't, if you will allow Him to. Don't be afraid of your uniqueness, rather present it to the Lord for Him to use as and when He needs to. We were not made in a sausage factory, we all have different personalities, experiences and talents that can be used to connect us to others. I am always so amazed how God matches people together; you start talking to them about your life and suddenly find out that they have experienced similar things to you. This is not a mistake or coincidence; this is a divine set up – a God-incidence!

Don't be scared to use the things about your life that are unique to reach the hearts of others and don't hold back from using your talents and giftings either. He truly can make all things work together for good, even those parts of your story that you are not proud of, He can use those to reach people's hearts. I have so many stories of how God has used natural things in my life to give me a stage for sharing the gospel. From using the tattoos on my arms and legs to reach a gang on the streets of the Bronx, to using my sense of humour to reach the lost at comedy nights; there are so many stories of how He has used every part of me!

> Don't be scared to use the things about your life that are unique to reach the hearts of others and don't hold back from using your talents and giftings either.

One particular moment involved a karaoke machine at a drunken party in rural Philippines. I was travelling with a team from my church to bless and encourage pastors in the smaller villages. They are faithful men and women who have given their lives for the gospel in very hard areas. Our heart was to bless the pastors but also try and lead as many as we could to Christ in every opportunity that arose. One afternoon we happened upon a small village in a very rural area; there was not much electricity and people lived very simplistically. After praying for the pastor and his family, the team sat down for fellowship with them. I heard some noise, so I left the team to find out what it was and where it was coming from. As I wandered down the dusty road, I came upon a group of around sixty people who were having a party in the street. They had wired a karaoke machine up to car batteries and were having a karaoke party! It was later on in the afternoon heat and they had obviously been drinking for a while. Then they spotted me. It did not take much for me to stand out in this community because they hardly ever had visitors from other countries. Intrigued by me as I stood and watched, a few people from the party came up to me offering me whiskey and whatever else it was that they were drinking. I politely declined. Then they told me I had to sing for them! If you know me then you know this made me smile on the inside. They did not know my life story, that for most of my early adult years I wanted to be Elvis Presley! I would often go around the bars singing rock and roll songs and had the dream of being an entertainer – no, let me be more honest: I wanted to be Elvis!

I had been used to singing in clubs and bars long before this moment, so I was more than ready! Looking through the song book I suddenly saw a track that I could use, "I Will Survive" by Gloria Gaynor. So, they pressed play and off I went. They seemed to be impressed and at the end I got over 80 on the machine's scoreboard; they loved that and applauded my performance. By this time my team had heard me giving it everything on this song and were now a part of this highly entertained crowd. I motioned my translator towards me and asked if I could say a few words; they agreed only if I would sing another song afterwards. I then shared for a few minutes a spontaneous message on how you don't need to just survive; God has a better plan than that! Then it came to my next song, so I flicked through the menu and there was the gem I needed: "My Way" by Frank Sinatra! Nodding at the man operating the machine, I began my next number. I am convinced that I felt God in it somewhere because I performed that song like I never had before! Finishing with an ending worthy of the Las Vegas stages, the crowd clapped and cheered, for I had hit the full 100 on the scoreboard. Oh, that had to be God.

Having well and truly got their attention now, I motioned to my translator and started to share a simple message on how God's way is better than "my way". I shared about how our own way can ruin our lives, but God's way restores our lives. Then I led them in a prayer, it was incredible, people were sobering up supernaturally as the Spirit of God moved them. Three quarters of the crowd accepted Jesus and gave their lives to Him! I released my team to pray for the sick and we moved around praying for people and watching people get healed and touched by the power of God. All this was to the amazement of the pastor who was watching with tears in His eyes. I was able to help connect him to this community that he had never been able to connect with. Afterwards he told me how he had tried and tried to connect with them but never could. Well, that afternoon God used a wannabe Elvis impersonator and an old karaoke machine that ran on car batteries to reach the unreachable. I tell you this story to encourage you that God wants to use your uniqueness, so don't you dare hide it away! If I had gone into the village judging them then they would not have listened. If I had got drunk with them then I would have disqualified myself. No, God had a unique plan for me that afternoon and He has a unique plan for you in the months that lay ahead too!

VIRTUAL EVANGELISM: REACHING THE WORLD FROM YOUR ARMCHAIR!

Never before in history has there been a window so large and so open for us to share the gospel with others and to see souls saved. Why is that? Because most of the world is now connected through one common thing: the internet. As of July 2020, 59 per cent of the world's inhabitants are active internet users. With the world more connected than ever, the internet is a very powerful tool for sharing our faith with others. The really sad thing is that many people choose to use this incredible tool to communicate things that hurt, tear down, and just waste time. The World Wide Web, with all its social media platforms such as Facebook, Instagram, YouTube and Zoom, are such powerful tools for sharing the gospel with others. Think about it: without even leaving your home, you have the ability to share your faith with a large percentage of the people that you know, and many who you don't know. The world is quite literally at your fingertips! With so many platforms now making video more readily available, you can even say it to them instead of writing it!

> What would the soul-winners from generations gone by have done with these tools?

This leaves me with a huge thought: what would the soul-winners from generations gone by have done with these tools? I can't even begin to imagine what men like Wesley, Finney and

Booth, the founder of the Salvation Army, would have done with this incredible ability to reach the world. But one thing I know for certain is that they would not have wasted or abused them. All they had in their time were pens and paper! Some didn't even have that, they just had quills, parchment, and candlelight, yet they reached multitudes. These great evangelists did their very best with what they had available to them and mobilised saints to carry the message of Christ to those who had not yet heard.

Some people might argue that these men would have had nothing to do with these modern-day, evil tools. That they would have disregarded them as being worldly. I would disagree. I think that, with both hands, they would have seized the opportunity to share the good news of Jesus through social media if it had been available to them. Yes, they probably would have been criticised for it and the religious people of their day might have deemed them "compromising", but I doubt that would have bothered them in the slightest. These were men and women who were consumed with God's mission and purpose for their lives and would have been more excited by the opportunity that these tools gave them to share the gospel than the nagging voices of the religious.

By daring to use these platforms to share the gospel, we are redeeming them for the purposes of God. A great example of this is the late evangelist, Billy Graham. It is recorded that Billy Graham received a lot of negative reaction from church folk when he chose to use a relatively new invention, called television, to reach millions. In the 1950s he regularly used radio, which was the internet of his day, to reach people. When television became widely available in the mid-1950s, many ministers claimed that it was evil. Yet

Graham grabbed the opportunity to share the gospel and he became the first preacher to use television to reach multitudes.

Again, I ask the question: what would Wesley, Finney, and Booth have done with the tools we have available to us today? It's too late for them to harness the benefits of the World Wide Web, but the good news is that it's not too late for us. Let's do what they would have done and choose to redeem these incredible soul-winning tools for the kingdom of God!

Before you even leave your house and physically speak to anyone, you have the ability to share your faith and let others know who Jesus is. I challenge you, soul-winner, to begin to use whatever social media you have and make it a part of your lifestyle evangelism. Why not start by sharing thoughts about Jesus, sharing verses that have spoken to you, or videos that talk about the saving grace of Jesus! Maybe even get a little bolder and go live yourself, letting your friends, family, and followers know why you choose to follow Jesus. Who knows what could happen? If enough of us did this we could create a virtual gospel revolution, if we would just choose to do with social media what Billy Graham did with radio and black and white television!

> we cannot put up random quotes about Jesus and expect them to speak to people if the rest of our online presence speaks something that is contrary to kingdom life

These are interesting days that we live in. They are just as the prophet Daniel saw when he said, "Many shall run to and fro, and knowledge shall increase" (Daniel 12:4). What an apt description that is of today. Knowledge has increased like never before. Just three decades ago no one had a mobile phone; phones were connected to walls. No one had heard of the internet, iPhones, or Google. It's like someone pressed fast forward on technology and the media. Take a good look around, we have so many wonderful ways of communicating with each other today, especially in the western world, it's ridiculous!

My question to you is a simple one: are you using these things and, if so, are you using them for good? Another key thought to ponder on this subject is: do you have a good online platform to speak to others from? I am of course speaking about your online etiquette and the reputation that you currently have on social media. Allow me to elaborate on this further and also lay some clear guidelines. Think about it this way, we cannot put up random quotes about Jesus and expect them to speak to people if the rest of our online presence speaks something that is contrary to kingdom life. Just as it is with real life, so it is with our virtual one! We have noted in previous chapters that for our words to reach others for Jesus effectively, we need to make sure that our lives are backing the message we speak; it is crucial that our witness is beyond just our words. We need to monitor our online presence also so that God can use our voice over these incredible communication platforms. What do I mean? Simple: be careful what you post or what you validate with a "like".

> **it is crucial that our witness is beyond just our words**

Think twice before posting things on your sites that could send out a conflicting message. Treat your virtual life like your real one and watch your witness online!

USE YOUR FREEDOM OF SPEECH WHILE YOU HAVE IT!

Freedom of speech is the fundamental right of all people. It is the right to be able to express what you love and feel strongly about to others, and includes your right to have a voice on social media. This is a liberty that we have all enjoyed to some degree, especially in the west, but sadly I believe that a day is coming sooner than we think when this freedom will become more and more restricted. A person's right to freely share what they believe will slowly be dissolved and restricted as it becomes wrapped up in politically correct red tape. This red tape's agenda is to silence people, especially the people who want to speak about God. Without trying to be a prophet of doom, just a realist, I believe that we will begin to see this happen more and more from this point on, not just on social media but also in other areas of life too. On that day when we are no longer allowed to share our faith as openly as we have been able to, let us not look back and say that we should have spoken louder when we could. May we not regret not having done more to protect our freedom to share Jesus with others. Rather, let us now seize the open doors and the opportunities that we still have available to us and use them to shout loudly to this world that Jesus saves! Even as I am writing this book, I am very aware of new restrictions and censoring that are now silencing people on social media platforms. While the door is still open to share the good news of salvation online, we must use it with everything we have; get posting, get sharing, and make Jesus known!

"The simple definition of evangelism: Those who know, telling those who don't."

Leith Anderson

CHAPTER 6

Knowing Your Message!

*For I am not ashamed of the gospel of Christ, for it is
the power of God to salvation for everyone who believes,
for the Jew first and also for the Greek. For in it the
righteousness of God is revealed from faith to faith; as it is
written, "The just shall live by faith." (Romans 1:16-17)*

This verse from the Apostle Paul is like a clarion call to
share the good news of what Jesus has done for us
unashamedly to all. When I read it my heart cheers! But
strangely enough, at the same time I find within myself a kind
of disagreement, as the question arises, "Is the gospel just good
news?" No, I don't believe it is! I believe the word "gospel",
which means "good tidings" or "a good message", is far too
small a description. When you truly understand what Christ
achieved through His death, burial, and resurrection, it is so
much better than just good news. It would be better described
as being great, amazing, phenomenal, mind-blowing, or
life-shaping news – not just good! Even these words do not
come close to correctly describing salvation, but they at least

come closer. If your gospel is merely good, with a small "g", then you have never fully unpacked it to see the true magnitude of all that it contains.

A correct perception, or revelation, of the message of Christ and the cross is vitally important to us as soul-winners because it will not only affect what we experience as followers of Jesus, but also the message that we share with others!

> A correct perception, or revelation, of the message of Christ and the cross is vitally important to us as soul-winners because it will not only affect what we experience as followers of Jesus, but also the message that we share with others!

Allow me to say this bluntly, if you don't know the fullness of what a great salvation it is that you have received, how are you going to communicate its correct weightiness and life-transforming depth to those you are speaking to? The writer of Hebrews puts it in a great way:

> We must pay the most careful attention, therefore, to what we have heard, so that we do not drift away. For since the message spoken through angels was binding, and every violation and disobedience received its just punishment, how shall we escape if we ignore so great a salvation? This salvation, which was first announced by the Lord, was confirmed to us by those who heard him. (Hebrews 2:1-3 NIV)

In the journey we have taken together in this book we have placed a great emphasis upon being commissioned and sent.

My prayer is that you now feel equipped, ready, and excited about winning souls, especially those in your Jerusalem. It is vitally important for us to now take some time to look at the message we are going with, lest we run with great zeal and great passion but actually deliver a lesser or, God forbid, even a false message to those we are looking to reach. This would actually waste the commitment that you have made to go and the passion you use to do so. There is a great biblical example of this in 2 Samuel 18:19-32 that is worth some reflection. As we read these verses, we see that David's general, Joab, needed to get some news to King David. This was important news concerning both the winning of a battle and the death of Absalom, David's son. A young messenger called Ahimaaz begs to be the one who runs with the message, but Joab pushes him aside, knowing that he did not know the full message. Joab says to the young messenger that this would not be his time, but he could run another time with another message. Joab gives the message to the Cushite to deliver instead. Still, the young messenger begs and begs to run, so eventually Joab says that he could run, knowing that he had sent the message already with a more reliable runner. In his zeal

> Ahimaaz had much zeal, which was good, but he did not have the full message that David needed.

Ahimaaz overtakes the Cushite and meets David first. David was excited to receive good news concerning the battle but when he asks the runner for information about Absalom, Ahimaaz doesn't know the information. In fact, he had to confess that he did not have the full message, just a couple of good bits that he had overheard. Then the Cushite arrives, who had actually been sent with the message and he explains to David everything he needed to know. You see, Ahimaaz had much zeal, which was good, but he did not have the full message that David needed. Let us not be like Ahimaaz with the message that Jesus has entrusted us to give to the lost! Rather, we must have the passion and great zeal of Ahimaaz but also be carrying the full message, lacking nothing.

Let's take a moment at the close of this book to consider our message so that in our going we can have a full assurance that what we are sharing contains the power of God to change a person's life and, indeed, their eternal destiny. In the hour in which we now live, where there are sadly so many other false or partial gospels and other competing philosophies made up of worldly wisdom in circulation, we who have been entrusted with the truth must know what we believe. We must be confident in our knowledge of all that God has done for us and given us through His only beloved Son, Jesus. It is vital that we have a healthy, well informed, and correctly balanced doctrine (understanding) of salvation. We each must have an ongoing commitment to be a person who, as Paul put so well, knows how to rightly divide the words of truth that God has committed to us.

> *Keep reminding God's people of these things. Warn them before God against quarrelling about words; it is of no value, and only ruins those who listen. Do your best to present yourself to God as one approved, a worker who does not need to actually be ashamed and who correctly handles the word of truth. (2 Timothy 2:14-15 NIV)*

The Message translation amplifies it so well, encouraging us once again that we should also live out the message that we are bringing.

> *Concentrate on doing your best for God, work you won't be ashamed of, laying out the truth plain and simple. Stay clear of pious talk that is only talk. Words are not mere words, you know. If they're not backed by a godly life, they accumulate as poison in the soul. (2 Timothy 2:14-18 MSG)*

We should all have an ongoing daily commitment to studying the Word so that we know what we should know, as we should know it (1 Corinthians 8:2). But this should not be arduous learning or something we struggle with because the subject is not abstract in nature, it's personal. It's simply learning all about someone we are now in relationship with and discovering what He has done for us. Another reason it does not need to be difficult is because we have the great teacher living in us. The Bible reveals that the Holy Spirit is present now in us to lead us into understanding all that is true in a way that it becomes enlightened revelation to us.

> *However, when He, the Spirit of truth, has come, He will guide you into all truth; for He will not speak on His own authority, but whatever He hears He will speak; and He will tell you things to come. He will glorify Me, for He will take of what is Mine and declare it to you. All things that the Father has are Mine. Therefore I said that He will take of Mine and declare it to you. (John 16:13-15)*

> *[I] do not cease to give thanks for you, making mention of*
> *you in my prayers: that the God of our Lord Jesus Christ,*
> *the Father of glory, may give to you the spirit of wisdom*
> *and revelation in the knowledge of Him, the eyes of your*
> *understanding being enlightened; that you may know*
> *what is the hope of His calling, what are the riches of the*
> *glory of His inheritance in the saints, and what is the*
> *exceeding greatness of His power toward us who believe,*
> *according to the working of His mighty power which He*
> *worked in Christ when He raised Him from the dead*
> *and seated Him at His right hand in the heavenly places,*
> *far above all principality and power and might and*
> *dominion, and every name that is named, not only in this*
> *age but also in that which is to come. (Ephesians 1:16-21)*

God's Spirit, heaven's great teacher, is now resident in your life and will be leaning over your shoulder, not to rebuke you but to help you understand. All you need to do is simply acknowledge Him and ask Him to help you every time you read God's Word, believe me when I say that He will! He wants you to gain revelation of the things you need to know more than you want to know them. Happy learning!

KNOWING YOUR MESSAGE

This section will now discuss an essential aspect of sharing the gospel, which is knowing the gospel! This could also be called "soteriology". Don't let this big word frighten you, "soteriology" simply means "the doctrine of salvation". It defines what a person should know about what salvation is, what it involves, and what it produces.

So, what are the fundamental truths that you must

understand about your doctrine of salvation? There are a number of vitally important details that you must communicate so that those who are listening can experience a full salvation that transforms their lives. This is a huge subject that could, in itself, take another book to explain comprehensively. But here are some of the key things that I believe a person's understanding of the gospel should include. In the next section I will break these apart and focus more on having a correct understanding of the message. However, it is important that you know what those key points are to make in that moment when you have limited time and are sharing the gospel with someone. The Billy Graham Evangelistic Association have written an incredible four-step guide to sharing the gospel, which you can find below. By memorising this pattern of sharing the gospel, it will ensure that you are not like that zealous messenger who only gave a partial message. This isn't everything they should know in their entire Christian life, but it is everything they need to know in order to be saved!

To share the gospel, you can follow these four simple steps:

1. Tell them about God's plan – peace and life. God loves you and wants you to experience the peace and life He offers. The Bible says, "For God so loved the world that He gave His only begotten Son, that whoever believes in Him should not perish but have everlasting life" (John 3:16). He has a plan for you.

2. Share our problem – separation from God. Being at peace with God is not automatic. By nature, we are all separated from Him. The Bible says, "For all have sinned and fall short of the glory of God" (Romans 3:23). God is holy, but we are human and don't measure up to His perfect standard.

We are sinful, and "the wages of sin is death" (Romans 6:23).

3. Talk about God's remedy – the cross. God's love bridges the gap of separation between you and Him. When Jesus Christ died on the cross and rose from the grave, He paid the penalty for your sins. The Bible says, "'He himself bore our sins' in his body on the cross, so that we might die to sins and live for righteousness; 'by his wounds you have been healed'" (1 Peter 2:24 NIV).

4. Our response – receive Christ. You cross the bridge into God's family when you accept Christ's free gift of salvation. The Bible says, "But as many as received Him, to them He gave the right to become children of God" (John 1:12).

To receive Christ, a person needs to do four things:

- Admit you're a sinner.
- Ask forgiveness and be willing to turn away from your sins.
- Believe that Christ died for you on the cross.
- Receive Christ into your heart and life.

Romans 10:13 says, "Whoever calls on the name of the Lord shall be saved." Here's a prayer you can pray to receive Christ:

"Dear Lord Jesus, I know I am a sinner, and I ask for Your forgiveness. I believe You died for my sins and rose from the dead. I trust and follow You as my Lord and Saviour. Guide my life and help me to do Your will. In Your name, amen."[2]

It's that simple; this is the message that you will bring! It's not complicated, anyone could understand it, even a child. The gospel really is as simple as this!

CLOSING THE DEAL

As well as sharing a correct and well-balanced message of salvation with a person, it is also vitally important that we always try our very best to "close the deal" with them! What do we mean by this? Closing the deal simply means to give someone the opportunity to pray the prayer of salvation with you. It will always be their decision as to whether they want to or not, but we should always as a soul-winner give them the opportunity! As a younger man I spent some time in sales, and in sales training a person is taught over and over again the importance of "closing the deal". A salesperson is taught to present the product they are selling in the best and most professional way that they can, making it highly desirable and beneficial to the potential customer. Then, they are taught to show the customer its availability and how they can have it for themself. These two steps are both key, but the third step is the most important, unless your goal is to only tell people about your product and offer it to them. While this is a very nice thing to do, there are no commissions attached to that because nothing is actually sold.

In the real world of sales an effective salesperson is taught that the final thing that they are to always do is to try and close the deal. They must ask the person: "Would you be interested in buying what I have shown you, and would you like to buy one today?" The potential customer is then left with a choice of responses: either, yes, no, or maybe later.

In many ways, as soul-winners, we follow the route of

what has been taught to people in sales, though we are not peddling something natural rather offering them something divine. Yet the steps they take are the same for us. As an effective soul-winner you must let the person you are talking to know who Jesus is and what He has done for them, then you must let them know that His salvation is available for them also. But then, like the salesman, we must take a moment to try and close the deal (initiating reconciliation) between them and God by asking: "Would you like to receive Jesus by praying a simple prayer with me?"

Just like with the salesman, you will normally hear one of those three answers. If their answer is yes, then do not waste a moment! Lead them in a simple prayer that invites Jesus into their life. They could say no, this is their right; if they say no then thank them for listening and encourage them to contact you if they ever change their mind. They could also say maybe. This normally means they like what they have heard but would like to hear more from you, or maybe they would like some time to think about what you have shared with them. This is not a negative response; it is the response of someone who is seeking and is probably not far from the kingdom (Mark 12:34). With this person you should make a plan to talk again and let them know that you are keen to keep talking to them and to continue hearing their questions. Like I said, you cannot determine which of those three responses a person will choose, but you can leave your encounter with them knowing that you did what God asked of you by offering them the opportunity of salvation. When we communicate the gospel to another person correctly it is like we lay a beautiful table for feasting. After doing so, it would be strange not to invite the person to eat, right?

Soul-winner, never be afraid to ask a person you have been sharing the gospel with if they would like to pray and receive Jesus. Giving them information about Him is good but inviting them to receive Him is better! What's the worst that could happen? They could say no thank you, or maybe later! I doubt that they are going to publicly flog or stone you in the marketplace, and in my experience most people are thankful that you cared enough to ask them. If you want to be an effective soul-winner, meaning that you are someone who sees souls saved, then be a soul-winner who not only shares the gospel, but also asks the all-important question, "Would you like to pray with me and receive Him?"

> Giving them information about Him is good but inviting them to receive Him is better!

UNDERSTANDING YOUR MESSAGE

It is important to know the message that we are sharing, but also to understand the message that you are sharing. In order to have dialogue with others, especially people of other faiths or belief systems, you are going to need to have clear answers for what you believe. In this next section I have taken a number of key points about salvation that we need to understand. I have briefly explained them and have included a couple of relevant scriptures. For those of you with an appetite to study these subjects in more depth I have included a study guide of key verses relating to each subject that will deepen your knowledge of each one. You can find this guide at the back of the book in the resource section.

These points can be a great tool for you to use when discipling someone, or yourself. You can use these as a way to unpack that box that they have received, called salvation. All of this doesn't need to be translated in depth at the moment of someone receiving salvation, but it should be, if possible, explained and unpacked soon after so that they know the fullness of what they now have. These are not points that will eventually be earned, or levels that can be achieved, rather they are all parts of what has already been received in salvation. Now is the time to uncover and explore those things in greater detail.

> When it comes down to it, everything about this good news starts, ends, and continually orbits around the love of God.

So, make sure that you have a good understanding of these things yourself and if you have led someone to the Lord then sit with them and talk through these points with them so that they do not lack anything!

THE LOVE OF GOD

> *For God so loved the world that he gave his one and only Son, that whoever believes in him shall not perish but have eternal life. (John 3:16 NIV)*

> *This is love: He loved us long before we loved him. It was his love, not ours. He proved it by sending his Son to be the pleasing sacrificial offering to take away our sins. (1 John 4:10 TPT)*

The gospel message that we share must always house God's

divine and never-ceasing love at the very core of it. When it comes down to it, everything about this good news starts, ends, and continually orbits around the love of God. It is essential that you convey the deep love of God for the person who you are sharing the gospel with. This includes His desire that no one, including them, would perish (2 Peter 3:9).

It was for nothing less than a love relationship that mankind was originally made in Adam and for nothing less than this that they are restored back to Him in Jesus. Love, to God, is not merely an action or something He occasionally does, rather it is who He is (1 John 4:8). We choose to love but He cannot help Himself, because it is Himself! In all things, including even His justice, His love is present because it is part of His nature.

> It was for nothing less than a love relationship that mankind was originally made in Adam and for nothing less than this that they are restored back to Him in Jesus.

The Bible announces to us that this creator God, who is love, could not and would not stop loving mankind even after they had fallen through their disobedience and rebellion. It was because of His unwavering love for us that He sent His only beloved Son to redeem us back to Himself (John 3:16). God's love is lavish (1 John 3:1) and through this lavish love He fully restores us back to being the children in His family that we were destined to be. Therefore, His love brings us from separation into sonship. All this was done while we were still unworthy sinners who were not deserving of it and having done nothing to warrant it (Romans 5:6-8). The ultimate demonstration of God's love is forever seen in Jesus hanging upon the cross for man's sin.

Stop and think deeply about it for a moment: how much must God love us (a fallen humanity) that He would provide the costly and unprecedented sacrifice of His only beloved Son to restore us back to Himself and to the life He originally designed for us to know? The incredible love of God must always be central, never just peripheral to the message we share with others, as it remains the motivation behind all He did for us and all that He still does for us today.

There is no shortage of verses in the Bible on the subject of God's love. Study them, memorise them and be sure to always include them when speaking to people about Him because it is His love that changes everything! Just as hymn writer Isaac Watts penned in his hymn "When I Survey the Wondrous Cross", it is indeed a "love so amazing, so divine" it "demands my soul, my life, my all"!

THE GRACE OF GOD

The Word became flesh and made his dwelling among us. We have seen his glory, the glory of the one and only Son, who came from the Father, full of grace and truth. (John 1:14 NIV)

For it is by grace you have been saved, through faith – and this is not from yourselves, it is the gift of God – not by works, so that no one can boast. (Ephesians 2:8-9 NIV)

"Amazing Grace, how sweet the sound that saved a wretch like me, I once was lost but now I'm found, was blind but now I see". (John Newton)

Because of God's unwavering love for us He extends to us, in Christ, an abundance of grace (Romans 5:17). It is because of this divine grace alone that a person can know the fullness of salvation and a perfect reconciliation with God. Grace explained simply is: God giving us what we don't deserve.

God's grace is His unmerited, unearned, and undeserved favour shown to man. It cannot be purchased or earned; it can only be freely received through His goodness and kindness. His grace is never based on, or given according to what a person deserves, rather upon them receiving, in Christ, what they do not deserve. As stated so clearly in Ephesians 2, it is by grace alone that a person is saved, through faith. Salvation is never based on man's achievements, performance, rights, or entitlements, which leaves every person unable to boast.

His grace replaces all of man's dead works of trying to achieve a state of right standing with God and simply leaves them positioned as thankful recipients now in possession of something they could never have gained by their own merit or efforts. His grace qualifies the unqualified and brings the separated back into perfect union with the one who has never stopped loving them. As with love, be sure to study further the incredible subject of God's grace, making sure as with love, that it is never far away from the good news message you share with others.

THE MERCY OF GOD

Let us then approach God's throne of grace with
confidence, so that we may receive mercy and find grace

to help us in our time of need. (Hebrews 4:16 NIV)

But in your great mercy you did not put an end to them or abandon them, for you are a gracious and merciful God. (Nehemiah 9:31 NIV)

Grace and mercy are always found near to each other, they are like two best friends! In fact, mercy is the doorway to both finding and experiencing His grace. Just as grace is God giving us what we do not deserve, mercy is God choosing to not give us what we do deserve! The Bible teaches us that because of Jesus, God's mercy now triumphs over His judgement towards us (James 2:13). Mercy is also something that is good for us all to choose when we are dealing with others. We must always be ready to show mercy, knowing that He has promised us that as we show mercy to others we are blessed, and that He shows mercy to us (Matthew 5:7).

Don't misunderstand me, judgement remains a reality and the Bible clearly reveals that certain judgement awaits those who reject Jesus in this life. But equally, those who have chosen Jesus can know that they have now been both judged and fully punished already in Jesus (Isaiah 53:5).

The gospel loudly declares to man that "He took our judgement and bore our punishment upon himself". This was what was happening upon the cross in that moment when the sky turned black and the heavenly Father turned His back on His Son (Mark 15:33-34). We all deserved His judgement because all had sinned, but in Christ, His mercy has now triumphed over judgement. In the Old Testament, in the tabernacle, we see the mercy seat of God above the tablets of the law that judged and condemned man (Exodus 25).

For us who now live under a new and better covenant, His blood found its rightful place on the mercy seat before God on our behalf and mercy has triumphed for us over the judgement that was due us.

Telling people of an impending judgement to convince them to receive Christ is not wrong, yet we must also remember that the Bible teaches that it's the goodness or merciful kindness of God that leads a person to true repentance. Another way to say this is that it changes the way they think about Him (Romans 2:4). May the love, grace and mercy of God be very commonly used tools in your soul-winning toolbox.

SALVATION IS A FREE GIFT

> *For the wages of sin is death, but the free gift of God is eternal life in Christ Jesus our Lord. (Romans 6:23 ESV)*

> *But the free gift is not like the offence. For if by the one man's offence many died, much more the grace of God and the gift by the grace of the one Man, Jesus Christ, abounded to many. And the gift is not like that which came through the one who sinned. For the judgement which came from one offence resulted in condemnation, but the free gift which came from many offences resulted in justification. (Romans 5:15-16)*

Another incredible truth that we get to share with people is that this amazing manifestation of God's love, grace and mercy that we call salvation now comes to them as a free gift! His salvation can never be bought, nor can it be earned, it can only ever be received. Paul put it so well in Romans 6 when he says that the wages (rewards) of our sin is always death, but the free gift of God is His eternal life in Christ.

A person's salvation will always remain a grace gift from God that can only ever be freely received from Him. If it could be earned, in that moment it would cease being a gift and be reduced to merely a wage, a reward, or something that we deserved. Equally a person is never expected to give anything in return for it as this would reduce it from being a priceless gift to merely a trade-off. Rather, our message should invite a person to just receive their salvation as a gift from God that was given because of His great love for them and His desire to restore them back into relationship with Himself.

This principle is also true when it comes to receiving the gift of the Holy Spirit. He is also to be received without the need of arduous travail, struggle, or begging. He, too, is to be freely received. Both of these gifts, the gifts of salvation and the Holy Spirit, come into a person's life simply by acknowledging that God has made them available to them as gifts, then by asking the Lord for them, and finally by thanking the Lord for them as they are received by faith into their lives and possession.

Being that salvation is a freely given gift from God, always remember that He expects nothing in return for it. His joy is found in the person receiving the gift and then daily choosing to live in the good of it for the rest of their days. Finally, always remember that though free to us, it was certainly not cheap for Him. The giving of Jesus as full payment for our salvation was the most expensive gift ever given.

Note: When sharing about salvation being a free gift with others, you will often need to help them to bypass their "but I need to earn it" default setting so they can simply extend their arms to freely receive it as the gift it is from the Lord to them.

FORGIVENESS OF SIN

> *And Peter said to them, "Repent and be baptised*
> *every one of you in the name of Jesus Christ for*
> *the forgiveness of your sins, and you will receive*
> *the gift of the Holy Spirit. (Acts 2:38 ESV)*

> *Therefore, my friends, I want you to know*
> *that through Jesus the forgiveness of sins is*
> *proclaimed to you. (Acts 13:38 NIV)*

This gift of salvation that He freely gives to us contains everything that a person needs or could ever need! It includes such things as the restoration of man's righteousness, eternal assurance, and experiencing a true joy and peace beyond anything they have ever known before. The list of benefits could carry on and on. It is indeed the "gift that keeps on giving", ever unpacking itself further and further in a person's life! Unlike other false religions and faiths that offer a measure of reward, or status, at the end of a person's lifelong pursuit, the Bible tells us that we receive

> The Bible tells us that we receive everything we are ever going to get from God the moment we believe. After that, we spend the rest of our lives working out and unpacking all that we received.

everything we are ever going to get from God the moment we believe. After that, we spend the rest of our lives working out and unpacking all that we received. A key thing for us to make clear to others when presenting the good news of the gospel is that it starts with the forgiveness of sin! By this do we mean the sins that they may have personally committed during the course of their life? Yes! But also, and in many ways more significantly, the sin nature they inherited in Adam. The plain truth is that we are all born into this life as sinners who were fully disqualified from relationship with God, even before we did anything wrong ourselves. Yet through faith in Jesus we can become forgiven saints who can stand fully forgiven and justified in His presence.

The very moment that a person believes in and receives what Jesus achieved for them at the cross, their sin is removed from their account! How far is it removed? According to Psalms 103:12 "as far as the east is from the west". This is a very interesting measurement to use because it is a continual measurement that has no ending point to it. This reveals that our sins are truly forgiven and forever lost in the bottomless ocean of His forgiveness, forever out of His sight as they remain cast behind His back (Isaiah 38:17). Let us also never forget the incredible promise in Hebrews that God made to all of those who would come through His Son into a new covenant relationship with Him, He promised that He would "forgive their wickedness and . . . remember their sins no more" (Hebrews 8:12 NIV). This is an echo of what He also said through the prophet Isaiah when He promised to blot out our transgressions for His own sake and remember our sins no more (Isaiah 43:25).

Seriously, what greater news could there be than this? God

totally settles the debt of the sinner! He does this by bringing them through the sin-separating death and burial provided in Christ, where He causes the sinner to die and the sin to be no more! In doing this, He deals not only with the fruit of sin in a person's life but also with the root, or factory, that was producing it, that being the old sinner with a sin nature that we were! He does this so that a person is able to come without hindrance into the brand-new life He has for them. I told you this was great news, didn't I? Keeping it really simple, if Jesus made full payment for sin then sin is now paid in full for those who have placed their faith in Him!

> Keeping it really simple, if Jesus made full payment for sin then sin is now paid in full for those who have placed their faith in Him!

A common question that people have around this subject is: what if I sin after I have received His forgiveness for sin? One answer to this question that I often like to use is that Jesus paid for all sin for all men for all time when He died two thousand years ago (Hebrews 10:12). This means that past, present and future sins were paid for at the cross. Now think about this: how many of your sins were future ones when He died for them 2000 years ago? All of them, right? Thanks be to Jesus that all sins were included in His one-time sacrifice for sin.

Another relevant thought to bear in mind when we speak to others about the forgiveness of sin is what John tells us in 1 John 1:9. He teaches that if we sin, or blow it, which we all do, then all that we are to do is simply confess it and, as we do, He remains ever faithful to both forgive and cleanse us from it in that very moment we pray. The simple principle here is that sin confessed is sin forgiven! Isn't that also wonderful news? At the cross, Jesus made total provision for all sin by His death. He has also made a way for us to be able to keep a clean conscience regarding sin through the simple confession of sins to Him who is now our high priest. Hebrews says that Jesus, our high priest, is able to empathise with our weaknesses and has made a way for us to come with boldness to receive God's grace and mercy whenever it is needed (Hebrews 4:14-16). The issue of sin, that thing that once separated people from God, has been settled by God and we are no longer called to live continually sin-conscious, rather, God-conscious.

Sin confessed is sin forgiven.

THE BLOOD OF JESUS

> *Knowing that you were ransomed from the futile ways inherited from your forefathers, not with perishable things such as silver or gold, but with the precious blood of Christ, like that of a lamb without blemish or spot. (1 Peter 1:18-19 ESV)*

> *From Jesus Christ, who is the faithful witness, the firstborn from the dead, and the ruler of the kings of the earth. To him who loves us and has freed us from our sins by his blood. (Revelation 1:5 NIV)*

This forgiveness of sin that is available to us is totally based on the blood that Jesus shed on the cross for us two thousand years ago. The message of the shedding of His blood must always remain central to our understanding of how the gospel works and can never be just extra. Under the old covenant (agreement between God and man), sin was forgiven, or put a better way, it was covered, because of the shedding of the blood of innocent animals such as lambs. For under the law without the shedding of blood there could be no forgiveness for sin (Hebrews 9:22). Yet the blood of animals which was sacrificed by the priests in the Old Testament could only ever cover sin and never fully remove it. When Jesus came as the spotless lamb that God himself provided, He allowed His blood to be shed for the removal (taking away) of sin (John 1:29).

An easy way of understanding this better is to use the example of carried debt on a credit card. If a person has a debt on a credit card and does not have the finances to clear that debt then they would choose to make minimum payments. These payments would not settle the debt, they would just cover it so that the provider of the card cannot prosecute them. Their ultimate desire would obviously be to not just make payments on the debt but to see it paid off in full. Yet, if they did not have the resources or ability to make total payment on their debt then a monthly minimum payment would be their only other option. In the same way, under the law (old covenant) the blood of animals was sacrificed which made a minimum payment on man's sin-debt. This gave man what they needed temporarily to continue to walk with God and know His favour. However, God had a much better long-term plan than this! His plan was for total sin-debt cancellation for man, which is what the shedding of the blood of Jesus (the lamb provided by Himself) achieved for us. The precious blood of Jesus shed at Calvary totally cleared our sin-debt so that no payment was left outstanding and nothing more was required. Hebrews paints the picture of the difference between Old and New Testament sacrifices in a very clear way; take a moment to read these verses.

> *For since the law has but a shadow of the good things to come instead of the true form of these realities, it can never, by the same sacrifices that are continually offered every year, make perfect those who draw near. Otherwise, would they not have ceased to be offered, since the worshippers, having once been cleansed, would no longer have any consciousness of sins? But in these sacrifices there is a reminder of sins every year. For it is impossible for the blood of bulls and goats to take away sins.*
>
> *And every priest stands daily at his service, offering repeatedly the same sacrifices, which can never take away sins. But when Christ had offered for all time a single sacrifice for sins, he sat down at the right hand of God, waiting from that time until his enemies should be made a footstool for his feet. For by a single offering he has perfected for all time those who are being sanctified. (Hebrews 10:1-4 and 11-14 ESV)*

Note the incredible finality found within the last sentence, that carries a present tense reality regarding a person who now believes. He has "perfected them by His one-time sacrifice"! The obedience of Jesus in going to the cross and the blood that He shed for us upon it is everything that was needed to cancel our sin-debt and set us completely free (Revelation 1:5).

The good news is that the blood of Jesus has not lost its power and by it people are still saved, healed and restored today. Robert Lowry summed it up so well in the words of a hymn that he wrote: "What can wash away my sin? Nothing but the blood of Jesus. What can make me whole again? Nothing but the blood of Jesus. Oh! precious is the flow, that makes me white as snow; no other fount I know, nothing but the blood of Jesus."

AN INVITATION OF RECONCILIATION

Not only is this so, but we also boast in God through our Lord Jesus Christ, through whom we have now received reconciliation (Romans 5:11 NIV)

All this is from God, who through Christ reconciled us to himself and gave us the ministry of reconciliation; that, in Christ God was reconciling the world to himself, not counting their trespasses against them, and entrusting to us the message of reconciliation. Therefore, we are ambassadors for Christ, God making his appeal through us. We implore you on behalf of Christ, be reconciled to God. (2 Corinthians 5:18-20 ESV)

This soul-winning message that we share with others is actually an invitation! An invitation to reconciliation. In successfully dealing with the issue of sin that once separated people from Himself, there remains now nothing that can stop a person from being reconciled (re-joined in relationship) to Him if they will simply place their faith in the reconciler, Jesus. According to 2 Corinthians 5, you and I are now God's ambassadors on the earth who carry a very special message and invitation that He has entrusted with us to share with every single person we meet who is yet to know Him. This message is the good news of what Jesus has achieved for them at the cross and if they will just place their faith in Him then all their former trespasses are forgiven and will no longer be counted against them. This invitation now beckons them to come and know the God who made them and welcomes them back into relationship and friendship with Himself; His arms are wide open. Reconciliation in its purest form is simply the act of bringing people back together again. The coming back into agreement of separated people and things.

Our invitation is a simple yet very profound one that reveals how God both took the initiative and paid the price to remove the argument (sin) that blocked a person from being able to return to Him so that now they can! Every wall of division that once separated man from God and prevented this reconciliation has now been pulled down and completely dismantled by Jesus. Good news: God is no longer angry with the person who places their faith in His Son. Upon receiving His gift of salvation, a person can walk in friendship with God completely free from any fear or expectation of His judgement or wrath coming upon them. Instead, they may now know His favour and providence.

THE WRATH OF GOD SETTLED

Let no one deceive you with empty words, for because of these things the wrath of God comes upon the sons of disobedience. (Ephesians 5:6)

For God did not appoint us to suffer wrath

> *but to receive salvation through our Lord*
> *Jesus Christ. (1 Thessalonians 5:9 NIV)*

Allow me now to take a moment to bring further clarity concerning the subject of the wrath of God, as it is again a subject that has been misunderstood by some. It is important for us to underline what God's Word teaches concerning the wrath of God in regard to the person who has received Christ and also the person who has not. John 3:36 says, "Whoever believes in the Son has eternal life, but whoever rejects the Son will not see life, for God's wrath remains on them" (NIV). The one who believes in the Son will not suffer God's wrath for his sin, because the Son took God's wrath upon Himself when He died in our place on the cross (Romans 5:6-11). But those who do not believe in the Son, who do not receive Him as Saviour, will be judged on the day of wrath (Romans 2:5-6). The message that we carry offers a person the certain salvation from God's wrath. Just as Noah's message to his generation was one that invited people to join him in the ark to escape the flood of God's judgement and wrath that they were due. Similarly, our invitation to reconciliation with God offers an escape and freedom to our generation from any wrath that they were previously due.

> Jesus took God's wrath towards us upon Himself on the cross. He Himself has become the ark that our generation needs to enter into in order to be saved.

Jesus took God's wrath towards us upon Himself on the cross. He Himself has become the ark that our generation needs to enter into in order to be saved. When a person receives

Christ as their Saviour, they move from being what is termed in Ephesians a "son of disobedience", meaning that they are found in Adam, into being found in Jesus, the Son of obedience. There remains, as promised, no wrath for those who are found in Jesus! Our message and heartfelt cry to others is, in many ways, just as Noah's! It pleads with the person who is lost to come into the ark of Jesus to escape God's wrath.

THE DIVINE EXCHANGE

> *For our sake he made him to be sin who knew no sin, so that in him we might become the righteousness of God. (2 Corinthians 5:21 ESV)*

> *For you know the grace of our Lord Jesus Christ, that though he was rich, yet for your sake he became poor, so that you through his poverty might become rich. (2 Corinthians 8:9 NIV)*

When a person responds to the good news of Jesus, they become beneficiaries of divine exchange. The sin that once separated them from God had to be paid for, or to put it a better way, it had to be judged and punished. At the cross, God did exactly that! Jesus, carrying our sin, was judged, condemned, and punished both as us and for us. By placing faith in Him, we now receive and live in the benefits of this substitutional act of divine exchange.

An exchange is a very precise and calculated thing and there are always two or more parties involved in an exchange, as it was at the cross. The cross was an unprecedented moment of divinely inspired exchange, where in one moment of time the innocent became guilty so that the guilty could become innocent.

Think about a time that you have exchanged something with someone. They left that moment of exchange with what was once yours and you left with that which formerly belonged to them, right? So it was at the cross. It happened in that one moment when Jesus died for everyone, and for us, as the other person involved in the exchange, the moment we believed and entered into the fruit of this divine exchange. Our gospel declares to man that 2000 years ago Jesus approached the cross innocent, blameless, and righteous (knowing no sin). On the contrary, we as a fallen humanity approached it guilty, totally to blame, and unrighteous (sinful). What later occurred on the cross, as the sky turned black, was the transaction of this incredibly divine exchange which was arranged by the Father (Mark 15:33-34). On the cross, Jesus became us so that we could become Him (placed in him). He took all of our sin, shame, and wickedness upon himself, which made full payment for it by His death and the shedding of His blood. But let us not forget that at the same moment the other half of the exchange, which was the purpose of God for the death of His Son, was taking place also. That other part was Jesus' righteousness, or right standing with God. The righteousness that He came to the cross with became fully ours!

> The cross was an unprecedented moment of divinely inspired exchange, where in one moment of time the innocent became guilty so that the guilty could become innocent.

This was again totally outside of the ability of our own performance, assistance, or involvement. All we did to become a partaker of the great benefits of this divine exchange was release our faith to believe and receive it. In simply doing this we were saved and made right (righteous) in the sight of God. When telling others about what Jesus has achieved for them it is key to let them see that it was all of Him with no percentage added by them. All that a person brings to this moment of exchange is their faith; this faith is also something inspired and given by the Holy Spirit (John 6:44)!

THE IMPORTANCE OF FAITH

For it is by grace you have been saved,
through faith. (Ephesians 2:8 NIV)

Therefore, since a promise remains of entering His
rest, let us fear lest any of you seem to have come
short of it. For indeed the gospel was preached to
us as well as to them; but the word which they
heard did not profit them, not being mixed with
faith in those who heard it. (Hebrews 4:1-2)

Another non-negotiable truth regarding a person receiving God's salvation is that it is the result of faith alone. God's Word reveals that it is impossible to please Him without faith (Hebrews 11:6) and that no one can be saved or receive the gift of salvation unless they come by faith, simply trusting as a child and gladly receiving it for the gift that it is (Matthew 18:3). As we have previously discussed, it is by God's mercy and grace that a person is saved, and they access His mercy and grace through faith alone. As the great Latin declaration that was spoken by saints of old, like Martin Luther, said so well, it's *sola fide*; faith alone!

Often when sharing the salvation message with others, they will feel they need to do something to qualify themselves for it. This most often springs from the works-based mentality that they were raised in that told them "nothing is free; if you don't do you don't get". Yet, this great salvation that God has provided for us totally violates this earthly principle and comes to us in a completely different way. It cannot be earned, traded, or begged for – only received.

"What must a person do to be saved?" A man once asked Paul. "Just believe in Him," was his response (Acts 16:30-31). Simply by placing their childlike trust in what He has said He has provided causes salvation. This remains totally independent from the need of any other man-made thing to assist it! I am speaking specifically of man-made religious works such as penance that places emphasis upon what a person does or seeks to add something to God's salvation. Think about the thief on the cross who was present with Jesus in the last moments on earth, without any time to change or reform His life. He called across to the Lord and asked if He would remember him when He comes into His kingdom. In asking this of Jesus, contrary to the mocking thief on the other side of Jesus, he places his faith in Jesus. I am so glad that we don't hear Jesus respond, "You have left it too late", or "Sorry, friend, I see you are earnest but you have not left enough time to prove you mean it". Rather, the Lord turned to him and said, "Today you will be with Me in Paradise" and within moments he was (Luke 23:43).

Faith remains another key aspect of your salvation message. We must uproot and replace the deceptions of other gospels that people have heard that told them how they must work to become saved. Freely He gives and so freely we must receive. Finally, let me also underline that it is not faith that saves a person, as faith is merely a trigger of response, it is the person placing their faith in Him that saves them and causes them to become a partaker of this great salvation also.

THE NEED FOR TRUE REPENTANCE

> *From that time Jesus began to preach, saying, "Repent, for the kingdom of heaven is at hand." (Matthew 4:17 ESV)*

> *Repent, then, and turn to God, so that your sins may be wiped out, that times of refreshing may come from the Lord. (Acts 3:19 NIV)*

Often when you hear people speaking about sharing the gospel you will hear the word "repent", and how there is a need for repentance in the life of a person who comes to God. But what does it mean to repent? Repentance is certainly an interesting and very important word regarding a person's correct approach to God and His kingdom, but often it is again a very misunderstood word. It is vital that we understand what the Lord is expecting of a person when He says that they are to repent. You see, the Old Testament and New Testament definitions of repentance can be very different. In the Old Testament, the word "repent" meant "to judge oneself, to have a mournful sorrowfulness" and "to breathe heavy in deep remorse". Whereas the New Testament word that is used by both Jesus and Paul is the Greek word *metanoeō*, which means "to think differently or reconsider". It calls for a person to change the way they think. I certainly believe that when a person comes to Jesus in true repentance there is a degree of mournful sorrowfulness or judging oneself for things, they have done wrong as the Holy Spirit reveals their true heart condition. But this is to be a doorway into something much bigger, which is a willingness to change their thinking in order to receive His truth, will and ways. When Jesus said that a person had to repent to enter His kingdom, He was stating that a person would have to be willing to change the way they think because His kingdom operates in a completely different way from what they have experienced, trusted in, or lived by before. So, when we tell a person they need to repent, just as with Jesus, we are not asking for many tears; we are asking them to be willing to come into a whole new way of renewed thinking.

Over the years that I have been an evangelist I have had the privilege of witnessing many people coming forward in meetings to salvation calls. As their emotions were stirred, many were crying genuine tears of regret and remorse. But I have also sadly watched many of these same people then never actually change their ways. Some even drifted back into things the Lord delivered them from. In contrast, I have seen others come forward to the salvation message of Jesus with a soberness, or a seemingly non-emotional response, yet in that moment they experienced a total revolution in their life as they committed to change the way they thought about things and how they were going to live from that moment on. The need for repentance is another key ingredient of the message we share with others but let us be sure that what we are expecting from people as they do it is what God is expecting of them also. Please know that I am not saying that there will not be tears or emotion when a person comes to Christ, because often there are, but this must also be accompanied with lasting transformation by a willingness to think differently from that point on. Think differently about what? About everything!

Repentance is not just about turning from something but also a turning towards something. In repenting a person turns from a previous way of thinking and living towards a brand-new way of living and thinking, a way that is now in full submission to the will of God for their lives. Understanding that they are now to submit their will to the will of God is a key ingredient in the decision they are making.

RIGHTEOUSNESS RECEIVED

> *For I am not ashamed of the gospel of Christ, for it is the power of God to salvation for everyone who believes, for the Jew first and also for the Greek. For in it the righteousness of God is revealed from faith to faith; as it is written, "The just shall live by faith." (Romans 1:16-17)*

> *But now the righteousness of God apart from the law is revealed, being witnessed by the Law and the Prophets, even the righteousness of God, through faith in Jesus Christ, to all and on all who believe. For there is no difference. (Romans 3:21-22)*

Paul's gospel message revealed the righteousness of God, and so must ours! Just like Paul's gospel, ours should clearly reveal the righteousness that comes from God. So, what is this righteousness that pleases Him and what does it mean for a person to be righteous?

To be righteous is to "be right". To be able to stand before God as innocent, accepted, and celebrated because your life is now fully right in His sight. It is vital that we understand that this righteousness we speak of is not self-righteousness, which means that we achieved it or earned it by our own ability. Rather, it is

> Paul's gospel message revealed the righteousness of God, and so must ours!

imputed, which means it has been added to us as a gift from God. It is a position that is given; never achieved.

> *For if, because of one man's trespass, death reigned through that one man, much more will those who receive the abundance of grace and the free gift of righteousness reign in life through the one man Jesus Christ. (Romans 5:17 ESV)*

Paul said of the good news he shared about Jesus that it was "powerful to save" because in it "righteousness from God was made known to man". A brand-new condition of right-standing with God, which is based upon faith and not achievements, works, or the law. The Bible, as a complete book, reveals two different types of righteousness: one which is based on a person's performance and a second that is imputed, or given. Referring back to the Old Testament and old covenant for better context, we see that under the law (the old covenant) a person's righteousness was totally based on what they did and their ability to keep the laws and requirements God had given through Moses. In doing this, a measure of righteousness could be obtained for a moment but was never able to be sustained with any permanence in a person's life because they were unable to successfully keep the law that produced it. To break just one law would mean a person was guilty of breaking them all and had to start again (James 2:10). We also know through other teachings given by Paul that the actual purpose of the law was only ever to lead a person to Christ (Galatians 3:24). Trying to keep the law would only ever cause a person to realise that they are totally unable to achieve it in their own ability, thus revealing to them their need for a saviour.

In the New Testament a new righteousness is revealed to us that is not based upon man's performance but totally on the finished work of the cross. Through the cross, Jesus completely fulfilled (not removed) the law which enabled God to be able to position a person's life in the risen Christ, the righteous one. So that now being "in Him", His righteousness would become their righteousness; a righteousness that pleases Him (Galatians 3:27).

The foundational truth concerning a person being in Christ from the moment they believe is another very key truth and one that should be threaded through all the other aspects of our salvation message. Outside of Christ we all have sinned and fallen short of what He expects or requires (Romans 3:23). "None is righteous, no, not one" (Romans 3:10 ESV), and all a person's good works in order to be righteous are as filthy rags in His sight (Isaiah 64:6). Yet in Him (Jesus) a person finds perfect forgiveness, justification, and sanctification, which leaves them spotless with Jesus' own righteousness. When the Father sees them, He sees the righteousness of His Son because their lives are now "in Him", which is all of Him and removes any prideful boasting on our end.

> *It is because of him that you are in Christ Jesus,*
> *who has become for us wisdom from God – that*
> *is, our righteousness, holiness and redemption.*
> *Therefore, as it is written: "Let the one who boasts*
> *boast in the Lord." (1 Corinthians 1:30-31 NIV)*

JUSTIFICATION

> *Yet we know that a person is not justified by works of the*
> *law but through faith in Jesus Christ, so we also have*
> *believed in Christ Jesus, in order to be justified by faith*
> *in Christ and not by works of the law, because by works*
> *of the law no one will be justified. (Galatians 2:16 ESV)*

> *For there is no difference; for all have sinned and fall*
> *short of the glory of God, being justified freely by His*
> *grace through the redemption that is in Christ Jesus,*
> *whom God set forth as a propitiation by His blood,*
> *through faith, to demonstrate His righteousness, because*
> *in His forbearance God had passed over the sins that were*
> *previously committed, to demonstrate at the present time*
> *His righteousness, that He might be just and the justifier*
> *of the one who has faith in Jesus. (Romans 3:22-26)*

As it was with mercy and grace, so it is again with righteousness and justification. They are always found together because they are interrelated. We see clearly in the verses above that the righteousness we now have, as new creation believers, is the result of our justification, which is something that once again comes through faith alone. These verses read like a harmony of all of the different aspects of salvation we have now spoken of coming together. To be justified is to be made just, or put even simpler, to become "just as if you never sinned".

Without allowing Himself to become unjust, God has legally justified us by carrying out the requirements of justice for what we deserved upon His Son Jesus who stood in our place as a substitutionary sacrifice. Jesus received for Himself the punishment that we were due, and that was the full payment for the sin of mankind. At the cross, God poured out the wrath and judgement that we deserved upon Jesus. In His death, Jesus settled the requirement of God for justice regarding the disobedience of Adam and the sin of mankind. This leaves us, the ones who were once guilty, now innocent and justified (just as if we had never sinned). Jesus, in His obedience even unto death, restored the peace between God and man which opened the way for a person to know Him and stand in His grace, fully justified. This is not something that will happen, but rather it is something that has happened; it is a past tense reality for the person who has placed their faith in God for salvation. Read these next verses from Romans 5 slowly, and fully digest this powerful past tense reality of what Jesus has provided for us.

Therefore, since we have been justified through faith,
we have peace with God through our Lord Jesus Christ,
through whom we have gained access by faith into
this grace in which we now stand. And we boast in

the hope of the glory of God. (Romans 5:1-2 NIV)

As with our imputed righteousness, God is not looking for us to achieve our justification any longer but rather to live from it, now being a reality in our daily lives. We live no longer to sin but to glorify Him. He is and always will be the One who is both just and the Justifier of those who place their faith in Christ.

REDEMPTION

In him we have redemption through his blood,
the forgiveness of sins, in accordance with the
riches of God's grace. (Ephesians 1:7 NIV)

For you know that it was not with perishable things
such as silver or gold that you were redeemed from
the empty way of life handed down to you from your
ancestors, but with the precious blood of Christ, a lamb
without blemish or defect. (1 Peter 1:18-19 NIV)

When we understand that Jesus shed His precious blood to justify us and make us righteous, then we can fully embrace the concept of our perfect redemption. Redemption can be another one of those "Christian" words that might initially feel like it could be quite difficult to understand. Yet its meaning is very simple and very powerful. Redemption simply means "to redeem", and to redeem something means to buy it back or to regain possession of something in exchange for payment. This is exactly what the Lord did when He died for us on the cross.

A great example of redemption is when something that has been stolen is returned to its rightful owner. This is certainly a relevant storyline to us as a lost and restored humanity! A brief overview of this storyline, which is found in Genesis, is that in the beginning mankind was created by God to belong to God. Mankind was fashioned by His loving hands for the most intimate of relationships between the Creator and His creation. But because of the disobedience of the fall of man that took place through Adam, mankind was taken from an inheritance of intimacy with God to becoming children of the devil. As the natural descendants of Adam, we were also partakers of His fallen nature – the very thing that produced a state of separation from God. Yet, God did not want man to be separated from Himself, or from experiencing His life, so He sent His only beloved Son to pay the required price for man's redemption. This price, one that was greater than anything that could be paid by man, was the blood of Jesus! Through the redemption that He secured for us, we are restored to the original intimate relationship that Adam knew before he was separated through his disobedience. The providence (protection and provision) of God also being restored to the person who has been redeemed. It is also good to note that this is not just something that affects a person in this life but it is also an eternal redemption in the life to come.[3]

> *He [Jesus] entered once for all into the holy places, not*
> *by means of the blood of goats and calves but by means*
> *of his own blood, thus securing an eternal redemption.*

3 For greater depth read *iamredemption* by Andy Elmes (Great Big Life Publishing, 2014).

> *For if the blood of goats and bulls, and the sprinkling of*
> *defiled persons with the ashes of a heifer, sanctify for the*
> *purification of the flesh, how much more will the blood*
> *of Christ, who through the eternal Spirit offered himself*
> *without blemish to God, purify our conscience from dead*
> *works to serve the living God. (Hebrews 9:12-14 ESV)*

NEW BIRTH

> *Jesus replied, "Very truly I tell you, no one*
> *can see the kingdom of God unless they*
> *are born again. (John 3:3 NIV)*

> *Praise be to the God and Father of our Lord Jesus*
> *Christ! In his great mercy he has given us new*
> *birth into a living hope through the resurrection of*
> *Jesus Christ from the dead. (1 Peter 1:3 NIV)*

The invitation contained within our message is not one of behaviour modification or the repair of an old life, rather it is the promise of a brand-new life and a totally fresh start! The unseen reality of a person's salvation is that, upon receiving Jesus as their Saviour, their old life ends and a brand-new one begins. It is just as if they are "born again". Other translations of the Bible say it in a number of other ways such as "born anew" or "born from above", but they all point to the same powerful truth, that a person is given a new beginning and a fresh start! This is the powerful reality of the new life that can be found in Christ, that God no longer knows a person by who they were, or by the sin nature they were once joined to.

You see, He didn't exchange His perfect life for us to experience a second-rate one! Rather, He gave His perfect life in exchange for our broken one so that we could experience a totally brand-new one. This new life is free from any history or a previous track record that the old one may have had.

The unseen reality of a person's salvation is that, upon receiving Jesus as their Saviour, their old life ends and a brand-new one begins.

The concept of a person being "born again" initially confused Nicodemus, the religious leader who Jesus was talking to in John 3. Nicodemus could not imagine how a man could return to his mother's womb a second time to experience a rebirth experience, especially now that they were fully grown. Many people who hear the message of second birth today might have a similar response to that of Nicodemus. Yet, what Jesus was actually saying was that it's not about an old life that is continued, recycled, or revived, but rather, a brand-new one is given with no history that can hold it back.

We all know that when a baby is born it does not struggle with its past, simply because it does not have one; everything is new. The plan of God by providing a new birth experience for those who believe in Him is to provide the same experience of a new-born baby. A new beginning and a past-less life is what God has in mind for our salvation experience. When studying the making of man in Genesis, we can see that the first man, Adam, was created on the sixth day as a fully grown being who had no previous history. Adam simply woke up to a wonderful new life that he had not known before. This is a wonderful type and shadow of when a person receives their new life in Christ, though they are not a baby naturally, the past that once defined them is washed away through a spiritual new birth experience. This provides a fresh beginning and a brand-new start for anyone and everyone who believes.

THE NEW CREATION

> *Therefore, if anyone is in Christ, he is a new creation; old things have passed away; behold, all things have become new. (2 Corinthians 5:17)*

> *Neither circumcision nor uncircumcision means anything; what counts is the new creation. (Galatians 6:15 NIV)*

From the very moment a person receives Jesus as Saviour and is born again, God regards them as a new creation. The person that they were passes away. We use the term "passed away" mostly around a graveside when a person is saying their final goodbye to someone who has died. So, what is meant when we say these words "passed away" at a funeral? It is the acknowledgement that we will never see that person on the earth again. This is exactly what Paul is teaching us regarding the new creation life that a person receives in Christ. The old man is crucified with Christ and in that moment, it is Christ who now lives in them and through them (Galatians 2:20). Just as it says so well in the NIV: "The old has gone, the new is here."

> The invitation contained in the gospel does not offer just behaviour modification; it offers a brand-new life!

The invitation contained in the gospel does not offer just behaviour modification; it offers a brand-new life!

God uses the power of an identification with death to facilitate the ending of one existence and the start of a new one. When sharing God's salvation plan with people, it is vital that we do not cause them to think that God is going to merely "patch them up" or "manage their rust"; He is going to do away with the person that they were so that they can be completely free to be a new creation. In their moment of salvation, among other things, a person undergoes a spiritual heart transplant, where God takes out of them an old heart and an old spirit and replaces them with a new heart and a new spirit which are His own (Ezekiel 36:26).

It is vitally important that a person understands what it means to become a new creation once they have been saved. If they do not understand the new creation, they will spend the rest of their lives trying to become something that they already are. Rather than doing that, they could spend their time living out of what God has already made them to be. As He promised He would, He has made all things new (Revelation 21:5).

> If they do not understand the new creation, they will spend the rest of their lives trying to become something that they already are

Note: Without changing any of the spiritual realities of what we have spoken about, it is also important to understand that after becoming a new creation and experiencing a new birth from God, a person can still be subject to certain natural consequences from things they might have done, or from the way they chose to live prior to their conversion. This is especially true if the things done had a negative effect on others or violated the natural laws of the land. It is key to understand that when balancing this reality. A person is unmistakably made new in the sight of God from the moment that they believe, and they have a blank sheet in regard to how they can now live in their future. However, there are certain natural consequences for things they might have done that they could still be outworking themselves. A great example of this would be someone who finds salvation while serving a sentence in prison for a crime they committed. The moment they believe in Jesus and are born again, the prison does not suddenly feel obliged to open the doors and let them go, even though they have now become fully set free on the inside of who they are. Sometimes there will be the natural need for ongoing restitution or consequence. Yet, even in these moments I have both seen and also have personally experienced how the Lord walks with us side by side through whatever we need to go through, always providing His supernatural grace, courage, and favour.

IDENTIFICATION

> For the love of Christ controls us, because we have
> concluded this: that one has died for all, therefore
> all have died. (2 Corinthians 5:14 ESV)

> We were buried therefore with him by baptism into
> death, in order that, just as Christ was raised from the
> dead by the glory of the Father, we too might walk in
> newness of life. For if we have been united with him

> *in a death like his, we shall certainly be united with*
> *him in a resurrection like his. We know that our old*
> *self was crucified with him in order that the body of*
> *sin might be brought to nothing, so that we would*
> *no longer be enslaved to sin. (Romans 6:4-6 ESV)*

What makes both the new birth and the new creation a living reality for a person is the way that God chose to bring it to pass. God did not just fake it, or just pretend to make a person new by overlooking who they actually were. Rather, He provided a real and effective death, burial, and resurrection for a person to experience without them having to provide it for themselves. You see, Jesus did not just die for us; He died as us! When a person comes to Jesus to receive their salvation, they are to, by faith, identify with His death, burial, and resurrection. By doing so, through the power of identification, this becomes their experience and testimony also. The plan of God was never to leave us as we were, but to bring us through a spiritual death and burial so that we could be totally free from who we used to be.

> **Jesus did not just die for us; He died as us!**

When communicating our understanding of salvation, it is vital that we do not lead someone immediately to their new life without first addressing correctly what preceded it! We must first lead them through the death and burial (disposal) of their old life, which comes simply by identifying with Jesus' death and burial. Sadly, a misunderstanding of this concept among so many believers today has meant that there are far too many "spiritual zombies" walking around. By this,

I am referring to people who don't fully know or cannot fully enjoy the new life that God has given them because they have never fully understood the fullness of death that they came through in Christ to gain it. I highly recommend investing some time to read through Romans 6:1-14. As you do, you will see the three powerful components: death, burial, and resurrection. It is when a person, by faith, identifies with each of these components that the power or significance of each of them becomes their personal reality.

> When communicating our understanding of salvation, it is vital that we do not lead someone immediately to their new life without first addressing correctly what preceded it!

First, His death means that we die in Him. Then, His burial means that our old life is buried with Him; it is done away with. Finally, His resurrection into newness of life by the Spirit, also becomes ours, in Him. The death He provides for us is not a morbid thing, rather it is something to celebrate because, by experiencing His death, a person is made free from everything old and the accusations of the devil. They are then able to enjoy a resurrected life, and not just in the life to come, but here and now also! Soul-winner, make sure that this liberating journey through death and into life is included in the gospel message you share so that they can walk away from who they were and everything that once had a claim on them. This way they can be, as Jesus said, "free and free indeed" (John 8:36).

Finally, in regard to this, it also remains true when we speak of identification that in coming to Christ for salvation we identify with the cross. The inclusion of the cross in our gospel presentation is again always a key thing for the listener as it reveals a place of separating for the person. In identifying with what Jesus achieved on the cross a person positions their lives spiritually upon it in Him. They are co-crucified with Christ!

> *I have been crucified with Christ and I no longer*
> *live, but Christ lives in me. The life I now live in the*
> *body, I live by faith in the Son of God, who loved me*
> *and gave himself for me. (Galatians 2:20 NIV)*

Another translation puts it even plainer when it says, "My old identity has been co-crucified with Messiah and no longer lives; for the nails of his cross crucified me with him" (TPT).

Obviously in preaching the cross we are not referring to the actual wooden object which was used being that it was no more than the executioner's tool of the day used to kill our Lord. Rather we identify with and boast in the crucifixion that occurred upon it. It is our identification with the crucifixion that separates a person from the world (natural realm) they knew to now be fully His.

> *My only boast is in the crucifixion of the Lord Jesus, our*
> *Messiah. In him I have been crucified to this natural*
> *realm; and the natural realm is dead to me and no*
> *longer dominates my life. (Galatians 6:14 TPT)*

MADE FULLY ALIVE

> *But God, being rich in mercy, because of the great*
> *love with which he loved us, even when we were*

> *dead in our trespasses, made us alive together with*
> *Christ – by grace you have been saved – and raised us*
> *up with him and seated us with him in the heavenly*
> *places in Christ Jesus. (Ephesians 2:4-6 ESV)*

> *When you were dead in your sins and in the*
> *uncircumcision of your flesh, God made you alive with*
> *Christ. He forgave us all our sins, having cancelled*
> *the charge of our legal indebtedness, which stood*
> *against us and condemned us; he has taken it away,*
> *nailing it to the cross. (Colossians 2:13-14 NIV)*

When considering the new life that a person receives in Jesus, it is good to also understand the dead condition that they had prior to that. According to the verses above, before a person receives Jesus they are "dead in their sins". From reading this we can conclude that sin, in some ways, was a secondary issue to a person being dead! Our problem was not just that we needed forgiveness for sin, but we were dead and needed life. To understand the context of this, we must refer once again to Adam the first man. Adam was originally made fully alive in body, soul, and spirit. He became dead in spirit when he disobeyed God, and then experienced exactly what God had warned him about: separation from His life (Genesis 2:17). Though Adam then lived on in his body and soul, he was now as God said he would be: dead of Spirit. Both Adam and Eve were then dead to the true life of God. Because of

> **Our problem was not just that we needed forgiveness for sin, but we were dead and needed life**

this, all of their children were separated from God's life also because two spiritually dead parents could only produce spiritually dead children. We inherited this death when we were naturally born because we were born from Adam's lineage. To clarify this point even further: every person born naturally is born spiritually dead!

Yet, when a person places faith in Christ and receives His life, then they experience a new life as they become reconnected to the Spirit of God that Adam, through his rebellion, disconnected us from. In other words, they come alive! In that moment, God breathes again His *zoe* life into them and raises them from death into life. They will never die spiritually again. A person who places their faith in Jesus instantly moves from the death they inherited in Adam to a life they receive in Christ; a new resurrection life that is eternal.

ONE WAY TO GOD

> *Jesus answered, "I am the way and the truth*
> *and the life. No one comes to the Father*
> *except through me. (John 14:6 NIV)*

> *Salvation is found in no one else, for there is no*
> *other name under heaven given to mankind by*
> *which we must be saved." (Acts 4:12 NIV)*

Contrary to the common deception that says "all roads lead to God", the Bible emphatically declares to us that they don't and that only one road, or should I say person, leads a person to God. That person is Jesus, God's only beloved Son! It might seem polite, or even politically correct, to say that faith in any god, or other self-appointed messiah, can lead a person to God, but the truth is that they don't! There are many other doors with many other names on them which all claim to lead to a universal god, but only one door leads to the true God and it is Jesus. When some people hear the absoluteness of this gospel message, they might feel that it is a very narrow-minded way of thinking, which actually – it is! Jesus Himself instructed us that we are to enter through the narrow gate and warned us to avoid the broader one that leads to death.

> Contrary to the common deception that says "all roads lead to God", the Bible emphatically declares to us that they don't and that only one road, or should I say person, leads a person to God

Come to God through the narrow gate, because the wide gate and broad path is the way that leads to destruction – nearly everyone chooses that crowded road! (Matthew 7:13 TPT)

There is certainly a place in our modern life for respecting other people's beliefs about other roads to God. However, there is no place for including or validating such thinking in the message of salvation that you share with others. Make sure you keep it pure and that there is no amount of "cocktailing" in your gospel that would attempt to politely mix Jesus and the salvation that comes through Him, with any other additive! The truth remains that only one way leads a seeker to find salvation and reconciliation with God and that way is, and always will be, Jesus!

SHARING A FULL GOSPEL

> *While Apollos was at Corinth, Paul took the road*
> *through the interior and arrived at Ephesus. There*
> *he found some disciples and asked them, "Did you*
> *receive the Holy Spirit when you believed?" They*
> *answered, "No, we have not even heard that there is*
> *a Holy Spirit." So Paul asked, "Then what baptism*
> *did you receive?" "John's baptism," they replied. Paul*
> *said, "John's baptism was a baptism of repentance. He*
> *told the people to believe in the one coming after him,*
> *that is, in Jesus." On hearing this, they were baptised*
> *in the name of the Lord Jesus. When Paul placed his*
> *hands on them, the Holy Spirit came on them, and they*
> *spoke in tongues and prophesied. (Acts 19:1-6 NIV)*

> *"I baptise you with water for repentance. But after*
> *me comes one who is more powerful than I, whose*
> *sandals I am not worthy to carry. He will baptise you*
> *with the Holy Spirit and fire. (Matthew 3:11 NIV)*

The good news that we share with others should not just include the first baptism, which is in water and represents the death, burial, and the resurrection of a person into newness of life (Acts 2:38). It should also include the secondary baptism, which is of the Holy Spirit. This baptism was spoken of by John, the forerunner to Jesus, and Jesus Himself. It is the Holy Spirit who causes a person to be born again and regenerated at salvation, but in this second baptism the Holy Spirit also empowers a person to live out the new life they just received. Notice that in Acts 19 Paul was speaking to people who had received Jesus and had been baptised in water, yet He offered them another baptism experience. The second baptism was referred to by John as being a baptism of "Spirit and fire". At the moment of baptism in the Holy Spirit, God is able to live freely within a person and assist them to live His way.

Think of it this way: not only does God provide a new car (life) for us, He also provides a new driver. You see, the reality is that without a new driver, people will most certainly crash the new car (life) that He has given them, just like they did to the old one! God's provision contained in His plan of salvation has a much better option than that, which is the internal guidance and ability of the Holy Spirit.

> There is certainly a place in our modern life for respecting other people's beliefs about other roads to God. However, there is no place for including or validating such thinking in the message of salvation that you share with others

When communicating the gospel with others, make sure that you include the option of receiving the baptism of the Spirit, which comes through just a simple prayer. Then, encourage the person to realise that they are now a passenger in the car of their life and the Holy Spirit is in the driving seat. It is this that will enable them to do all the things they could not before (Philippians 4:13). Some soul-winners choose to leave out this very important facet of the message when leading others to Christ, but in doing so, they teach a partial gospel that leaves a person in a condition that was far less than what God intended for them. Without the indwelling ability of the Holy Spirit it often produces hypocrisy, guilt, and shame as someone tries to live out their new creation life in their own strength. Soul-winner, I charge you to share a full gospel not a partial one!

TRANSFORMATION

> But we all, with unveiled faces, beholding as in a mirror the glory of the Lord, are being transformed into the same image from glory to glory, just as by the Spirit of the Lord. (2 Corinthians 3:18)

> Stop imitating the ideals and opinions of the culture around you, but be inwardly transformed by the Holy Spirit through a total reformation of how you think. This will empower you to discern God's will as you live a beautiful life, satisfying and perfect in his eyes. (Romans 12:2 TPT)

We now understand that we do not carry a weak, man-made message of mere behaviour modification, where a person just receives a passport to heaven when they are saved but experiences no transformation in the life they now live. Rather, we testify of how God's Spirit and ability comes to live within the person that receives Him and causes them to not only experience a regeneration at their new birth (Titus 3:5), but also an ongoing transformation that occurs from the inside out. It is the working of the Holy Spirit that causes the transformation needed within a person. The role of the person is simply to yield to Him, while at the same time they must allow their minds to be renewed by God's

Word. It's here that we can see the stark contrast between the salvation that is offered by religion and the true salvation that is offered by God. With religion, a person is expected to change their behaviour from the outside to the inside. Religion places the responsibility on a person to modify their life by telling them to stop doing this, or to start doing that. This often produces suppression rather than transformation of things that need to be dealt with. This leads a person to a state of hypocrisy, as they pretend or live a lie in order to keep the people around them happy. Whereas, the true message of God speaks of a supernatural (beyond normal) change that occurs in a person that happens from the inside to the outside!

God intends that a person would choose to abide in the Word of God and yield to the leading and ministry of the Holy Spirit that lives in them. As they do, supernatural change will begin to take place that is radically above and beyond the natural ability of that person. The Greek word for "transformed" that is used by Paul in 2 Corinthians 3:18 is *metamorphoō* from which we get the English word "metamorphosis". It is also used in Romans 12:2 where it mentions the importance of renewing your mind with God's Word. This word *metamorphoō* describes the supernatural change that occurs on the inner, unseen part of something, which later breaks through the outer, seen part. A great visual demonstration of this transformation is when a caterpillar turns into a butterfly. Nothing is added, or changed externally, yet what appears from the cocoon after the metamorphosis takes place is nothing like what originally entered it! This is exactly what God planned for the transformation of people after their salvation; inside first and outside second.

God takes the responsibility, through His abiding Spirit, to bring about the transformational change that is needed in a person. All that we are called to do is to daily yield to what He is doing. I am so saddened when I encounter people who are desperately trying to be what God wants them to be in their own strength. They are always failing, or coming short, because this was never the plan of God for them. His plan was much simpler and far more effective! His plan is this: we give our lives to Him, then we receive His life and get to experience a new life breaking out. At new birth a person receives the incorruptible seed of God's life which then germinates in the fruitful soil of a hungry heart and causes a healthy life that looks like Jesus. Like a baby chick hatching from within an egg, a day comes when what God has grown and transformed within you breaks through the shell of everything you used to be, to His glory and not yours. All of this happens not by our might or ability but by His Spirit alive now in us (Zechariah 4:6).

For you have been born again [that is, reborn from above
– spiritually transformed, renewed, and set apart for His
purpose] not of seed which is perishable but [from that
which is] imperishable and immortal, that is, through the
living and everlasting word of God. (1 Peter 1:23 AMP)

THE KINGDOM OF GOD

Fear not, little flock, for it is your Father's good
pleasure to give you the kingdom. (Luke 12:32 ESV)

Therefore let us be grateful for receiving a kingdom that

cannot be shaken, and thus let us offer to God acceptable
worship, with reverence and awe. (Hebrews 12:28 ESV)

Our redemption message also offers a person citizenship to a brand-new kingdom – His kingdom! The kingdom of God is not far, far away, or just another realm that we hope to experience one day beyond the grave. Rather, as well as being in heaven it is also here on earth right now! When it says of Jesus that He went from village to village preaching the gospel, it actually says, "He preached the gospel of the kingdom" (Matthew 4:17; 9:35). Every place He went, He welcomed people to come into His kingdom and experience a superior way of living. When He ascended, Jesus did not take His kingdom with Him, for it was already in heaven. He left it here on earth, not in buildings but in people. His kingdom is not just among us but also within us (Luke 17:21). It is what He sent His first disciples to preach and now us also. The Bible actually reveals that it is the gospel of the kingdom that will be preached in every place before the end comes (Matthew 24:14). So, His kingdom is present now and should also be something that we share with others and invite them to come into.

It is when a person is born again that they come into His kingdom (John 3:5), but also, the kingdom comes into them. Think about it this way: Jesus is the King that we receive when we believe, so now, wherever there is a King, there is also His kingdom. The two are synonymous; to have one means you have the other also! When a person responds to the gospel, their lives are taken from an old kingdom, the kingdom of darkness, and they are translated into a new kingdom, the kingdom of the Son, Jesus (Colossians 1:13).

From that very moment they become citizens of His kingdom, and as they chose to live true to the grain of His kingdom and no longer the one that they knew before, they also become loyal subjects of it. In many ways this makes a person a dual citizen, doesn't it? They are still alive, which means they have a natural citizenship that is connected to their first birth, but they also have a second and more important citizenship through their second birth. Jesus Himself said of us in John 17:16 that we are no longer of the world we once knew, though He has left us in it for His purposes. We must remember that we are in it, but no longer of it. Romans 12:2 encourages us also concerning our new citizenship that we are no longer to conform to the ways of the world that we knew, but rather now be transformed by His kingdom way of life. 1 John 2:15 teaches us that we are to no longer love the things of the world like we once did but to now seek first His kingdom and its ways (Matthew 6:33).

When sharing the gospel, it is a good thing to also help people to understand this new citizenship that becomes theirs the moment they believe, so that they can begin to live true to its ways and the lordship of its King, Jesus. This new way of kingdom living can be so very different to the one they knew before. This is why it is vital for you to encourage them to get themselves positioned into a healthy church under a good spiritual pastor who can help them to be further discipled in understanding kingdom life and their walk with the Lord.

THE LORDSHIP OF CHRIST

For if we live, we live to the Lord, and if we die, we die to the Lord. So then, whether we live or whether

*we die, we are the Lord's. For to this end Christ died
and lived again, that he might be Lord both of the
dead and of the living. (Romans 14:8-9 ESV)*

*What good does it do for you to say I am your
Lord and Master if what I teach you is not
put into practice? (Luke 6:46 TPT)*

The subject of the lordship of Christ naturally follows on from the kingdom way of living we just spoke about. As we previously established, Jesus is the King of the kingdom to which they now belong. Another really good definition for kingdom that can help us to understand it better is simply "rule and reign". Prior to their new birth, a person belonged to the devil and, knowingly or unknowingly, they lived under his rule and reign. But when they are born again, this person is supernaturally translated into a brand-new rule and reign (kingdom) that is of the Lord Jesus. The devil no longer has any authority or any legal rights over the person, because these rights stopped the moment that they died in Christ!

When a person is saved, they do not become a law unto themselves, rather, they are to acknowledge and live under the lordship (rule and reign) of Jesus, the King of Kings and Lord of Lords (Revelation 19:16). This is not done in some religious or legalistic way, rather, in a relational and faithful way.

The person is no longer to serve the will of the devil or their own will as they formerly did but now submit their lives fully to God's will. For a person to correctly live under the lordship of Christ means that they now gladly submit their lives to His will. The Bible boldly announces to us that one day every knee will bow, and every tongue will confess that Jesus is Lord, but we, as His followers, gladly make the decision to do it now, from our own desire and choice. We recognise His rule and reign in the here and now, not just in heaven one day. The lordship of Christ is another key part that is often missing from some people's gospel message. Make sure that the acknowledgement of it is not absent from yours. Remember that it is not something that comes into play on the other side of the grave, but this side also. It is a reality the moment a person's life becomes His.

THE RETURN OF JESUS, JUDGEMENT, AND HELL

> *Therefore keep watch, because you do not know on what day your Lord will come. But understand this: if the owner of the house had known at what time of night the thief was coming, he would have kept watch and would not have let his house be broken into. So you also must be ready, because the Son of Man will come at an hour when you do not expect him. (Matthew 24:42-44 NIV)*

> *When the Son of Man comes in his glory, and all the angels with him, he will sit on his glorious throne. All the nations will be gathered before him, and he will separate the people one from another as a shepherd separates the sheep from the goats. He will put the sheep on his right and the goats on his left. Then the King will say to those on his right, "Come, you who are blessed by my Father; take your inheritance, the kingdom prepared for you since the creation of the world."*

Then he will say to those on his left, "Depart from me, you who are cursed, into the eternal fire prepared for the devil and his angels."

Then they will go away to eternal punishment, but the righteous to eternal life. (Matthew 25:31-34, 41, 46 NIV)

The return of King Jesus is something that every person should expect and should be ready for. Though the exact day or hour is not known by anyone (Matthew 24:36), we can be assured that His second coming is a certainty. The first time Jesus came, 2000 years ago, He came to save us and bring us into His kingdom. His second coming is not another mission to save but rather to collect those who belong to Him, His kingdom people. On the day of His return, which the Bible says will be as "a thief in the night", in a moment referred to by some as the rapture, those who are alive will be called up in the sky to meet Him along with those who have fallen asleep, meaning they have died.

Those who belong to Him (who received Him as Saviour), whose names are unblotted in the Lamb's book of life, will then be together with Him, not fearing or facing judgement or punishment for sin as this was already carried out upon them in Him when He was judged and punished on their behalf as their substitute. Yet, for those who have rejected Him and His offer of salvation in this life there remains an inescapable judgement to which the punishment is eternal separation from God in the place the Bible refers to as hell, a place of never ceasing torment. But it remains very important for us to remember when presenting these truths to others that God actually sends no man to hell! Rather, through His mercy and grace He has provided a way for every man to escape it and to instead experience eternal paradise with Him. Yet God will not violate the freewill He has given to man, as this would be unjust, so making the choice to experience a heaven with Him or a hell without Him in the life to come remains every person's choice. Oh, that we would share the gospel in a way that would persuade the heart of a person to choose eternity with Him!

These days, out of a desire for people to discover the love of God in a way that changes their life rather than just a fear of hell, we do not preach a message of "fire and brimstone" as many preachers of old once did. But let us never forget that hell flames still burn bright and an eternal separation from God remains true; it is a painful reality for every person who does not receive Christ. Let me underline that God, in His love and justice, has provided a way for every person to escape this eternal sentence, but it remains their choice to do so or not! On the other hand, the good news for a person who receives Jesus as their Saviour is that they have assurance of heaven being their eternal home. This assurance is steadfast because it does not find its strength or validity in our performance, rather in the perfect finished work of the cross. When sharing the gospel with others you have the permission of heaven to let them know that they can have this assurance also, all they need to do is as you have done and place their faith in the saving grace of Jesus.

As stated at the beginning, I have provided only a very brief synopsis or overview of what I believe are some of the key ingredients to a balanced understanding of what should be included in our theology of salvation. I am conscious that there also remain other related and interrelated subjects that are of equally important value. But to have a healthy understanding of the ones I have mentioned, I believe, will give you a full and effective toolbox to be the soul-winner He has called you to be. Don't forget that at the back of this book, in the resource section, there is also a key verse study guide with many relevant verses for each of the above topics to enable you to study them further. And I highly recommend my book *Breathe Again* to increase your understanding of what happened when you were born again.

WHAT YOUR GOSPEL SHOULD NOT INCLUDE!

We have looked at some key points that your understanding of the gospel should include but let us also take a moment to highlight some things that it should definitely not include. Paul was very stern about what he called "other gospels" and he gave very severe judgement to those who were preaching them. Why was he so hard on other gospels? Because he knew that a wrong or weak gospel could actually affect a person's salvation and potentially lessen their experience of the salvation that Jesus has provided for them.

He knew very well that a weak gospel would only produce weak Christians. He also knew that a compromised gospel would produce compromising Christians. And he knew that a wrong gospel would mean that people remained separated from God. Look at these verses where Paul speaks in more detail of some of these other gospels and false prophets.

> *I marvel that you are turning away so soon from Him who called you in the grace of Christ, to a different gospel, which is not another; but there are some who trouble*

*you and want to pervert the gospel of Christ. But even
if we, or an angel from heaven, preach any other gospel
to you than what we have preached to you, let him be
accursed. As we have said before, so now I say again, if
anyone preaches any other gospel to you than what you
have received, let him be accursed. (Galatians 1:6-9)*

*Preach the word! Be ready in season and out of season.
Convince, rebuke, exhort, with all longsuffering and
teaching. For the time will come when they will not
endure sound doctrine, but according to their own desires,
because they have itching ears, they will heap up for
themselves teachers; and they will turn their ears away
from the truth, and be turned aside to fables. But you be
watchful in all things, endure afflictions, do the work of
an evangelist, fulfil your ministry. (2 Timothy 4:2-5)*

Your soul-winning message should at all times be totally
Christ-centred and unpolluted from things such as:

*Man-made philosophies, fables, and wisdom
that find no root in Christ or in sound biblical
truth, but are based merely on worldly thinking
or human traditions (Colossians 2:8).*

Legalism – where God's love for you and your salvation
is earned by your performance and keeping laws or rules.
Universalism or the belief in a universal salvation. This
is an old heresy that regularly resurfaces in different forms,
with the purpose of deceiving people away from truth. It
teaches that all humankind will eventually be saved and in

heaven with God, whether or not they adhere to key biblical principles such as the need for personal repentance and acceptance of Jesus as Lord for a person to be saved. Among a list of other nice sounding errors, universalism teaches that Jesus paid for everyone at the cross meaning that everyone is saved and going to heaven. This a very subtle deception because it is true that Jesus paid for everyone's salvation at the cross, but it is also true that this salvation is activated individually in a person's life when they personally place faith in Him. Universalism often teaches about the mercy and grace of God but ignores God's justice. It celebrates that many roads lead to God rather than just Jesus.

Dead works. These are pointless deeds and unnecessary ceremonies, performances and procedures that are done to gain what has already been freely given to a person when they place faith in Christ (Hebrews 9:14).

Man-made religious additives which purpose to get things from God or attempt to get God to do the things we want Him to do. These include such things as the teaching of penance, Hail Marys, indulgences, and the worship of Mary, the saints, or angels. These include the worship of any statue or idol made by or in the image of man. It is Christ alone who is to be worshipped. None of these other things have any credible biblical reference to support them but find their origins in man's misperceptions of God and His salvation rather than in God's revealed ways.

> If you can't back it with the Word of God correctly then don't share it! Always keep it based on Jesus and what He achieved for us!

These are a few examples of things that should not be a part of the gospel you share with others. The main key is to keep it biblical! If you can't back it with the Word of God correctly then don't share it! Always keep it based on Jesus and what He achieved for us! The gospel is such an unlimited and multi-faceted message that we should never need to add anything to it. When others choose to share things that are only trendy, or catchy, to appease the itchy ears of people, then you must remain committed to what is the truth, the whole truth, and nothing but the truth. By doing so, you will have the assurance that what you have shared contains the very power of God to save the life of the person you're speaking to. Remember that we are carriers of a message that has the ability to take a person from separation from God into a restored relationship with Him, as well as re-routing them from a certain lost eternity to a guaranteed life in heaven.

FALSE PROPHETS (FAKE MESSENGERS)

Watch out for false prophets. They come to you in sheep's clothing, but inwardly they are ferocious wolves. By their fruit you will recognise them. (Matthew 7:15-16 NIV)

There are many warnings in the gospels and the New Testament about false prophets and false gospels. This was a problem when the gospel was first being preached and it is still a problem today. People who preach partial truth, or total lies that are driven by ignorance, deception, or selfish gain. As Jesus revealed so well, you will recognise these false prophets by the fruit of their lives. This world, specifically our generation, needs us to carry the true message to those who desperately need to hear it. If false prophets have purposely decided not to remain silent with their counterfeit gospels, then we cannot be quiet with the genuine one that God has entrusted to us. Today there are people all around us who are desperate to hear the truth about God and the salvation He has provided. So purpose today to be a proclaimer of His undiluted truth. It is time for the Church (people of God) to rise to their feet as a mighty army of messengers, who are carrying His good news.

"To be a soul winner is the happiest thing in the world. And with every soul you bring to Jesus Christ, you seem to get a new heaven here upon earth."

Charles H. Spurgeon

Epilogue

We have finally reached the end of our journey into lifestyle evangelism. I hope and pray that our time together, within the pages of this book, have both motivated you to go and equipped you to feel confident in your going. I hope that you feel the heartbeat of God for the lost in a new way and have a fresh, Holy Spirit inspired fire now burning within you to see the lost saved. The Lord has indeed given us everything we need to be the soul-winners He has called and commissioned us to be, now set your heart on going! We no longer need to hide behind church walls or old excuses, but we can stand up and join the army of soul-winners that are arising in this hour to go into the harvest field and see it won for the Lord.

My prayer is that you will know His boldness and His ability as you step out to be the witness that He has called you to be. Also, that you would experience the empowerment of the Spirit every time you open your mouth to share Jesus with another person. Finally, soul-winner, please allow me to send you into your harvest field with a commissioning prayer:

Heavenly Father, I thank You for this precious saint who has decided to be a soul-winner. Fill them afresh with Your Spirit, Lord. Empower them to be an effective witness in their Jerusalems, and in every other place that their feet might go. Thank You for freedom from every fear and a heavenly boldness from this day on, to share Jesus with others. May they experience Your leading, Holy Spirit, and Your gifts flowing through their lives in a powerful way. Give them souls for their labour, Lord, so that they would one day hear You say, "Well done, good and faithful servant." Kingdom come, Lord, kingdom come. Amen.

NOW, GO!

God always makes his grace visible in Christ, who includes us as partners of his endless triumph. Through our yielded lives he spreads the fragrance of the knowledge of God everywhere we go. We have become the unmistakable aroma of the victory of the Anointed One to God – a perfume of life to those being saved and the odour of death to those who are perishing. The unbelievers smell a deadly stench that leads to death, but believers smell the life-giving aroma that leads to abundant life. And who of us can rise to this challenge? (2 Corinthians 2:14-16 TPT)

Resources

Key Verses for a Deeper Study of Soteriology

THE LOVE OF GOD

Psalm 52:1, John 3:16, John 15:13, John 16:27, John 15:9, Luke 11:42, Romans 5:8, Romans 5:5, Romans 8:35, Romans 8:39, 2 Corinthians 13:14, Galatians 2:21, Titus 3:4, 1 John 2:5, 1 John 3:1, 1 John 3:16, 1 John 4:7-10, 1 John 4:16, 1 John 4:18-19, Ephesians 2:4, John 15:12, Ephesians 3:18-19, Psalm 103:11.

THE GRACE OF GOD

Luke 2:40, Acts 13:43, Acts 20:24, Romans 4:14-16, Romans 5:1-2, Romans 5:15, Romans 5:20-21, Romans 6:14, 1 Corinthians 1:4, 1 Corinthians 3:10, 2 Corinthians 6:1, 2 Corinthians 9:14, Galatians 2:21, Colossians 1:6, 2 Timothy 1:6, Titus 2:11, Hebrews 2:9, Hebrews 12:15, 1 Peter 1:10, 1 Peter 4:10, 1 Peter 5:12, Jude 1:4, Galatians 5:4, Ephesians 2:4-9, Hebrews 4:16.

THE MERCY OF GOD

Deuteronomy 7:9, Joel 2:13, Psalm 52:8, Romans 9:14-18, Romans 12:1, 2 Corinthians 1:3, 2 Corinthians 4:1, Galatians 2:21, Ephesians 3:1, Titus 3:4-5, 1 Peter 2:10, 1 Peter 5:12, Romans 11:29-31.

SALVATION IS A FREE GIFT

Romans 5:15-16, Ephesians 2:8, Matthew 10:8, Acts 8:20, 1 Corinthians 2:12.

FORGIVENESS OF SIN

Matthew 9:6, Matthew 26:28, Mark 1:4, Mark 2:10, Luke 1:76-77, Luke 3:3, Luke 5:24, Luke 24:46-47, Acts 2:38, Acts 5:30-31, Acts 10:43, Acts 13:38, Acts 26:18, Ephesians 1:7, Colossians 1:14, Hebrews 9:22, Hebrews 10:18, 1 John 1:9, 1 John 2:12.

THE BLOOD OF JESUS

Ephesians 2:13-16, Romans 3:24-25, Romans 5:9, Hebrews 9:22-26, Hebrews 10:1-19, 1 Peter 1:2, 1 John 1:7, John 6:53-56, Revelations 12:11.

AN INVITATION OF RECONCILIATION

Romans 5:10-11, 2 Corinthians 5:18-20, Hebrews 2:17, Colossians 1:20-22, Ephesians 2:14-16.

THE WRATH OF GOD SETTLED

John 3:36, Romans 1:18-19, Romans 2:5, Luke 3:7, Romans 5:9, Romans 12:19, Ephesians 5:6, Colossians 3:5-6, 1 Thessalonians 2:15-16, Revelations 14:9-10 & 19, Revelations 16:1, Revelations 19:15.

THE DIVINE EXCHANGE

Isaiah 53:5, Matthew 16:26, Mark 8:37, 1 Corinthians 15:20-21, 2 Corinthians 8:9, Galatians 3:18, Philippians 2:6-8, Hebrews 1:3, Hebrews 5:9, 2 Corinthians 5:21.

THE IMPORTANCE OF FAITH

Ephesians 2:8, 1 Corinthians 15:1-2, Galatians 2:16, Hebrews 10:39, 2 Timothy 3:15, 1 Peter 1:3-5, 2 Philippians 3:9, Thessalonians 2:13, Romans 1:17, Romans 4:5, Romans 3:22-26, Romans 4:11-13, Romans 9:30-32.

THE NEED FOR TRUE REPENTANCE

Matthew 3:2, Matthew 3:8, Matthew 4:17, Matthew 11:20, Matthew 18:3, Matthew 21:32, Mark 1:15, Mark 6:12, Luke 13:3-5, Luke 15:7, Acts 2:38, Acts 3:19, Acts 8:22, Acts 17:30, Acts 26:20, Romans 2:4, 2 Corinthians 7:9, 2 Timothy 2:25, 2 Peter 3:9.

RIGHTEOUSNESS RECEIVED

Matthew 5:20, Matthew 6:33, James 2:10, Philippians 3:7-9, Romans 3:10, Romans 4:1-13, Romans 5:17-19, Romans 6:18, Romans 10:1-12, Galatians 2:20-21, 1 John 2:29, 1 Peter 2:24, 1 John 1:9, Romans 14:17, Galatians 3:5-9, Matthew 5:6, Ephesians 2:8-9, James 2:23, Titus 3:5, Philippians 1:11, Ephesians 6:14.

JUSTIFICATION

Romans 3:20-24, Romans 3:28, Romans 4:22-24, Romans 5:1, Romans 5:9, Romans 8:30-34, Romans 9:14-16, Galatians 2:16-17, Galatians 3:8-11 & 21-24, Titus 3:7, 1 Corinthians 6:11.

REDEMPTION
Ephesians 1:7, Ephesians 1:14, Ephesians 4:30, Titus 2:14, Psalm 130:7, Romans 3:24, 1 Corinthians 1:30, Luke 21:28, Psalm 107:2, Colossians 1:14, 1 Timothy 2:6, 1 Peter 1:18-19, Galatians 4:4-5, Hebrews 9:11-12, Matthew 20:28, Psalm 49:7-8, Galatians 3:13, Hebrews 9:15, Psalm 111:9, Mark 10:45.

NEW BIRTH
John 3:3-7, Galatians 4:31, 1 Peter 1:3, 1 Peter 1:23.

THE NEW CREATION
2 Corinthians 5:17, Galatians 6:15, James 1:18, Colossians 3:10-11.

IDENTIFICATION
Romans 5:8-10, Romans 6:3-5, Romans 6:10, 1 Corinthians 11:26, 2 Corinthians 4:7-12, 2 Corinthians 5:14, Galatians 2:20-21, Philippians 3:10-11, Colossians 1:22, 2 Timothy 2:11.

MADE FULLY ALIVE
Hebrews 2:14, Romans 5:18, 1 Corinthians 15:22, 1 Corinthians 15:36, Ephesians 2:1, Colossians 2:13, 1 Peter 3:18, Romans 4:17, 2 Timothy 1:10.

ONE WAY TO GOD
Acts 2:21, Acts 4:12, John 14:6, Matthew 7:13-14, Luke 13:24, Acts 3:16, Romans 10:10, Galatians 3:26, Acts 16.30.

SHARING A FULL GOSPEL

Matthew 3:11, Mark 1:8, Luke 3:16, Acts 1:5, Acts 11:16, Matthew 28:19, Acts 2:38, Romans 15:18-19, 1 Thessalonians 1:5, Matthew 22:28, 1 Corinthians 2:4-5, 2 Corinthians 6:5-7, 2 Corinthians 10:4.

TRANSFORMATION

1 Samuel 10:6, Mark 9:2, Romans 12:2, 2 Corinthians 3:18, Titus 3:5.

THE KINGDOM OF GOD

Matthew 6:33, Matthew 11:11, Matthew 12:28, Matthew 19:24, Matthew 21:31, Matthew 21:43, Mark 1:14-15, Mark 4:11, Mark 4:26-30, Mark 10:14-15, Mark 10:23-25, Mark 12:34, Luke 6:20, Luke 8:1, Luke 9:2, Luke 9:60, Luke 17:20-21, Luke 18:29, John 3:3-5, Romans 14:17, 1 Corinthians 4:20, 1 Corinthians 6:10, Galatians 5:21, Hebrews 12:28.

THE LORDSHIP OF CHRIST

Ephesians 1:20-22, 1 Timothy 6:13-16, Romans 10:9-10, 1 Corinthians 12:3, Revelations 17:14, Revelation 19:16.

THE RETURN OF JESUS, JUDGEMENT, AND HELL

Luke 17:20-36,1 Thessalonians 4:13-17, 1 Thessalonians 5:1-5, 1 Corinthians 15:50-52, John 14:1-3, 2 Peter 3:7, Hebrews 9:27, Revelation 2:11, Revelation 20:15, Revelations 21:8.

FALSE PROPHETS
- Matthew 24:24, Matthew 16:11-12, Acts 20:28-30, 2 Peter 3:14-18, 2 Peter 2:1-22, 1 John 4:1-6.

How to Talk to Jehovah's Witnesses, Mormons, Atheists, and Muslims About Jesus

Not only is it important for you to know what you believe, but it is important to know what others believe too. As a soul-winner you will find yourself in conversations with people of all different belief systems. It is important that you know their fundamental beliefs so that you can properly combat the lies of the enemy. This short overview of just a handful of belief systems will equip you with the practical knowledge to share the gospel with people of other beliefs when you find yourself in those conversations.

The main points of difference between Christianity and other belief systems will usually be over these criteria:

- Who God is
- Who Jesus is
- How you can be saved

It is not as difficult to have a conversation with someone of a different belief system when you know what they believe about these three points. Following you will find a brief overview of what Jehovah's Witnesses, Mormons, Atheists, and Muslims believe, and then the key points of difference between them and Christianity, with relevant scriptures.

I hope that this resource will enable you to have a greater understanding of other belief systems so that you can be bold in sharing the gospel with them. Please do not use these ideas as points of argument, or ammunition for a fight, but rather as loving truths. Remembering always to do all things in love (1 Corinthians 16:14).

FUNDAMENTAL DIFFERENCES BETWEEN JEHOVAH'S WITNESSES AND CHRISTIANITY

Jehovah's Witnesses were founded in 1884. They were initially called Zion's Watchtower and Tract Society until they renamed themselves the Jehovah's Witnesses in 1931. They have a worldwide membership of around 9 million people in 205 countries. This is a relatively small number compared to Christianity's 2.3 billion, however JWs claim to be adding 200,000 members each year. They have their own interpretation of scripture which is called the New World Translation.

The fundamental difference between Christianity and JWs is that they don't believe that Jesus is who the Bible says that He is – one with God – but rather they believe that He is a created being. They also do not believe that He resurrected from the dead in bodily form. It is clear from 1 John 4:1-4 that "every spirit that does not confess that Jesus Christ has come in the flesh is not of God".

JW Beliefs	The Bible
Do not believe in the Trinity. JWs don't believe that God the Father, Jesus the Son, and the Holy Spirit are a triune being. Instead, they see Jesus as a created being who is important but is not one with the Father. They see the Holy Spirit as an impersonal force, not a person who is in the trinity.	It is clear through scripture that Jesus is one with the Father. *John 10:30* *I and My Father are one.* *Matthew 28:19* *Go therefore and make disciples of all nations, baptising them in the name of the Father and of the Son and of the Holy Spirit.* *Isaiah 9:6 NIV* *And he will be called Wonderful Counsellor, Mighty God, Everlasting Father, Prince of Peace.*

Believe that Jesus is Michael the Archangel.

They believe that Michael the Archangel, who is hardly referenced in the Bible, is Jesus. You can read that word for word on their website (https://www.jw.org/en/library/books/bible-teach/who-is-michael-the-archangel-jesus/).

They believe that Michael is another name for Jesus. That Jesus/Michael was the first created being.

Jesus is not a created being, or an angel, but He is one with God. He existed in the beginning with and as God. Quite simply: Jesus is God.

John 1:1-3 NIV
In the beginning was the Word, and the Word was with God, and the Word was God. He was with God in the beginning. Through him all things were made; without him nothing was made that has been made.

1 Corinthians 8:6 NIV
Yet for us there is but one God, the Father, from whom all things came and for whom we live; and there is but one Lord, Jesus Christ, through whom all things came and through whom we live.

Do not believe that Jesus resurrected in His physical body.	This is crucial in Christianity because we believe that we died, were buried, and resurrected in Jesus. The Bible is clear about the fact that Jesus rose again in bodily form on the earth.
	Luke 24:36 NIV *While they were still talking about this, Jesus himself stood among them and said to them, "Peace be with you."*
	1 John 4:1-3 *Beloved, do not believe every spirit, but test the spirits, whether they are of God; because many false prophets have gone out into the world. By this you know the Spirit of God: every spirit that confesses that Jesus Christ has come in the flesh is of God, and every spirit that does not confess that Jesus Christ has come in the flesh is not of God."*

Believe that only members of their Church will be saved and, of those, only 144,000 people will get into heaven.

The sad part is that they believe most of those spaces are already filled and so they can only hope that they might inherit the earth.

This comes from Revelation 7 where there are 144,000 from the tribes of Judah, 12,000 from each tribe. However, this is actually the 144,000 that God seals during the 7 years of tribulation to come. The Bible is very clear that anyone who calls on the name of the Lord will be saved and that it is God's heart that none would perish. The 144,000 VIP list is nonsense.

John 3:16
That whoever believes in Him should not perish but have eternal life.

1 Timothy 2:3-4
God our Saviour, who desires all men to be saved and to come to the knowledge of the truth.

Romans 10:13
For "whoever calls upon the name of the Lord shall be saved."

Do not believe in hell.	The Bible is clear that everyone who does not accept salvation through Jesus will experience eternal separation from God in hell.
They do not believe that there is a place where the wicked are tormented after death. They think it would be against the nature of God.	*Revelation 21:8 NIV* *But the cowardly, the unbelieving, the vile, the murderers, the sexually immoral, those who practise magic arts, the idolaters and all liars – they will be consigned to the fiery lake of burning sulphur. This is the second death.* *Matthew 25:41* *Then he will say to those on his left, "Depart from me, you who are cursed, into the eternal fire prepared for the devil and his angels."*

The amazing news that you have to share with them is that Jesus is God! He came to the earth in flesh, fully God and fully man, to die on the cross as payment for their sin! He then rose to life in the flesh. Everyone who calls on the name of Jesus is saved and has access to a relationship with their loving Father! They can continue to tell people about Jesus, not to earn a place in the 144,000, but because of the amazing gift that He has given them! Hell is a real place for real people and the only way out is Jesus.

It is important to note that many times when a JW knocks at your door, they are already trained in the art of verbal warfare. They will have answers to argue with but they will not be able to argue with love. If you engage in loving conversation then it will be more effective than a fight. Take the low road, use your scriptures, and love them with the love that Jesus has for them.

SOURCES

https://www.bible-knowledge.com/jehovah-s-witnesses/

https://en.wikipedia.org/wiki/List_of_religious_populations

https://www.jw.org/en/library/books/bible-teach/who-is-michael-the-archangel-jesus/

https://www.blueletterbible.org/study/cults/acts/acts_jw.cfm

https://www.bbc.co.uk/religion/religions/witnesses/beliefs/beliefs.shtml#:~:text=Witnesses%20believe%20that%20Hell%20(as,to%20torture%20humans%20for%20eternity.

FUNDAMENTAL DIFFERENCES BETWEEN MORMONISM AND CHRISTIANITY

Mormonism, or The Church of Jesus Christ of Latter-day Saints, is the largest sect in the world, with well over 16 million members worldwide. Mormonism was initiated in the 1820s by Joseph Smith in upstate New York. Today, the US continues to house the most Mormons of any continent, particularly in the state of Utah. Although a sect, Mormons widely self-identify themselves as a Christian religion. It is important to note that, although they see themselves as Christian, they are not one because their beliefs are not in line with any Christian religion. Their most sacred text is the Book of Mormon. However, they also believe in the Bible and two other texts.

Mormon beliefs about salvation differ enormously from the salvation of the Bible. Not only do they present a works-based salvation rather than a grace-based one, they also believe that they too can become gods. These beliefs come from their lack of grounding in the Bible as a result of the exaltation of the Book of Mormon. A fundamental truth of Christianity is found in Deuteronomy 4:2, "Do not add to what I command you and do not subtract from it, but keep the commands of the Lord your God that I give you" (NIV).

Mormon Beliefs	The Bible
Do not believe that God is an eternal being. They believe that God the Father was once a mortal man and then became God.	God is uncreated and eternal. He has been forever and will be forever, He is not a man. *Numbers 23:19 NIV* *God is not human, that he should lie, not a human being, that he should change his mind. Does he speak and then not act? Does he promise and not fulfil?* *John 4:24 NIV* *God is spirit, and his worshippers must worship in the Spirit and in truth.* *Revelation 1:8 NLT* *"I am the Alpha and the Omega – the beginning and the end," says the Lord God. "I am the one who is, who always was, and who is still to come – the Almighty One."* *John 1:1-3 NIV* *In the beginning was the Word, and the Word was with God, and the Word was God. He was with God in the beginning. Through him all things were made; without him nothing was made that has been made.*

Do not believe that God is the Trinity: Father, Son, and Holy Spirit. They believe that Jesus and God are separate beings.	God is a Trinity: Father, Son, Holy Spirit. He is one being that includes Jesus Christ. Jesus is God. *John 10:30 NIV* *I and the Father are one.* *Matthew 28:19* *Therefore go and make disciples of all nations, baptising them in the name of the Father and of the Son and of the Holy Spirit.*
Believe that the Book of Mormon is the most correct book on earth. Although they read the Bible, in their eyes it is secondary to the Book of Mormon. They believe in four sacred texts.	The Bible alone is the Word of God. It alone is the authority of Christian beliefs. No other book can take the place of the Bible. *2 Timothy 3:15-17 NIV* *And how from infancy you have known the Holy Scriptures, which are able to make you wise for salvation through faith in Christ Jesus. All Scripture is God-breathed and is useful for teaching, rebuking, correcting and training in righteousness, so that the servant of God may be thoroughly equipped for every good work.* *Deuteronomy 4:2 NIV* *Do not add to what I command you and do not subtract from it, but keep the commands of the Lord your God that I give you.*

Believe that salvation is eternal life and it is obtained through Jesus' atonement AND their own actions.

They believe that part of the work was done by Jesus so that all could have eternal life, but to receive the fullness of that they need to rely on their own works.

That "fullness" is called exaltation (godhood) and it means that if they keep all the Mormon teachings then eventually they too will become gods and have the same relationships with their spiritual children as God has with us. They will also receive all of the power, glory, dominion, and knowledge of God.

This is radically different to the salvation of the Bible, so that is why Mormonism is certainly not a Christian religion. Salvation is a free gift that was earned by Jesus' sacrifice. Through faith in Jesus alone we become saved and enter back into relationship with our creator God. By Jesus, we receive the free gift of eternal life with God. Our actions, or works, have nothing to do with adding to, or taking away from that gift of salvation.

We do not become gods if we work harder or keep the teachings precisely. Only God is God. We do good works and keep His Word only because we love Him. Love always equals obedience.

Ephesians 2:8-10 NIV
For it is by grace you have been saved, through faith – and this is not from yourselves, it is the gift of God – not by works, so that no one can boast. For we are God's handiwork, created in Christ Jesus to do good works, which God prepared in advance for us to do.

Romans 3:20 NIV
Therefore no one will be declared righteous in God's sight by the works of the law; rather, through the law we become conscious of our sin.

John 14:15 ESV
If you love me, you will keep my commandments.

When they come to your door, why not challenge their ideas? Instead of being afraid of them and their different beliefs, why not just prod and question what they actually believe? Chances are they will come up with some sort of formulated, text-book answer, but the questions will remain in their heart. Ask them about the validity of the Book of Mormon, ask them about why they believe Jesus is not God. Take the upper-hand of the conversation. They have come to your door to share about their beliefs, but any conversation has two sides, so share about your beliefs too.

WHAT THEY NEED TO KNOW:

No amount of works can increase or decrease your salvation. Jesus alone can give you salvation, and it is only through faith in Him that you are able to be saved. The Bible is the Word of God and no other text can be added to it. It is totally true, with no errors.

SOURCES

https://en.wikipedia.org/wiki/Mormons

https://www.namb.net/apologetics/resource/comparison-chart-mormonism-and-christianity/

https://uk.churchofjesuschrist.org/what-mormons-believe-about-jesus-christ

https://www.str.org/w/verses-for-your-conversations-with-mormons

https://www.bbc.co.uk/religion/religions/mormon/beliefs/salvation_1.shtml#:~:text=Mormons%20believe%20that%20human%20beings,also%20have%20work%20to%20do.

TALKING TO AN ATHEIST ABOUT JESUS

With atheists, it is not so much about what they do believe but what they do not believe. So rather than confronting difference in beliefs, let's look at some effective ways to talk to atheists about Jesus. Often when someone is an atheist, especially if they are a self-proclaimed atheist, then they have made that decision at one point in their life. Therefore, that is their belief system and it affects the way that they live their lives. In many cases, when someone says that they are an atheist, rather than just not having a belief, it is a firm belief in an absence of God.

CHOOSE A STORY RATHER THAN A DEBATE

Steer clear from the hostility of a debate. You don't have to tell them everything that you know and out-smart them; that is not your job! You can explain certain things, but don't try to win a fight with words. Instead, seek out the wider story of that person and how they came to believe what they believe. Every person has a story and there is a reason for the choices that we all make. So, how did they come to atheism? What led to this choice? When listening to their story you can begin to identify points of conflict with religious beliefs. This will give you more knowledge about where the person actually is with God than just accepting that they are a "brick wall" to God. Remember, it's not about winning the argument, it is about winning the soul.

FIND A POINT OF CONFLICT WITH A PERSON, SCENARIO, OR EVENT, AND SEPARATE THAT FROM CONFLICT WITH GOD

Many times the person you are speaking to may have had a moment of conflict with an influential person in their life. This could include a pastor, priest, parent, or friend. Something might have happened to them that caused them to question whether God was real. Identifying this point of conflict, by question-asking and by reliance on the Holy Spirit, will help you to get to the root of their unbelief and to heal that.

Whatever this moment of pain or disappointment was, it is important to make a separation from that moment and God. Perhaps they were let down by someone who was a Christian; you can remove that hurt from being dependent on God. Perhaps they weren't rejecting God, but rather a person or circumstance.

REMEMBER THAT HE IS NOT FAR FROM EACH ONE OF US

Even though it might seem like, on the outside, an atheist is far from God, remember to look with your spiritual eyes. The truth is that God is not far from each one of us, and we are each reaching out to find him (Acts 17:27). God is in control, and He appointed every step of each person's life; He set their boundaries and appointed their times. He is not afraid of that word, "atheist", so we shouldn't be either. Every person is looking for the truth, and you have it!

The God who made the world and everything in it is the Lord of heaven and earth and does not live in temples built by human hands. And he is not served by human hands, as if he needed anything. Rather, he himself gives everyone life and breath and everything else. From one man he made all the nations, that they should inhabit the whole earth; and he marked out their appointed times in history and the boundaries of their lands. God did this so that they would seek him and perhaps reach out for him and find him, though he is not far from any one of us. "For in him we live and move and have our being." As some of your own poets have said, "We are his offspring." (Acts 17:24-28 NIV)

RELIANCE ON THE HOLY SPIRIT

You have a tool that cannot be matched: the Holy Spirit! Allow Him to speak wisdom and knowledge to you that you could not otherwise know. Moments of supernatural, unexplainable power can give God the glory. By using the power that is available to you, you can turn someone's disbelief into belief in a moment. Just as one moment was able to cause them to question God, one moment can cause them to believe in Him!

FUNDAMENTAL DIFFERENCES BETWEEN ISLAM AND CHRISTIANITY

Islam is the world's second-largest religion, after Christianity, with around one quarter of the world's population. Islam was founded by the prophet Muhammad in the 7th century, in the Middle East.

It is important to understand the basic beliefs of Islam because of the number of Muslims that there are in the world! The number of Muslims in Europe is becoming increasingly larger, as it is the fastest growing major religion in the world, and so now is the time to understand how to speak to Muslims about Jesus!

Muslim Beliefs	The Bible
Believe that Jesus was a prophet sent to guide the Children of Israel. They believe He is a messenger of God, but not the Son of God. Jesus is a fundamental figure in Islamic theology; however, they reject the lordship of Christ. An interesting note is that one of Jesus' names in the Quran is "Word of God" (Kalimatu'llah).	The Bible is clear that Jesus is fully God. *John 14:9 ESV* *"Whoever has seen me [Jesus] has seen the Father."* *John 1:1-2 ESV* *In the beginning was the Word, and the Word was with God, and the Word was God. He was in the beginning with God.*

Consider the Trinity as a division of God's Oneness, which is a grave sin. That God's name is Allah.	The Bible shows that God is three in one: Father, Son, and Spirit. *Deuteronomy 6:4* *Hear, O Israel: The Lord our God, the Lord is one.* *John 10:30 NIV* *I and the Father are one.* The name of this Triune God is Yahweh
Believe that the Quran is the verbatim word of God. While Muslims believe that the Quran and the Bible are sent by God, they believe that the Bible is distorted/altered. One example of this is the crucifixion. Muslims do not believe that Jesus was really crucified, but rather that a substitute was crucified and Jesus hid until He could meet the disciples.	Christians believe that the Bible is the perfectly inspired Word of God. The crucifixion of Jesus Christ is a crucial element of Christian theology because His death was the atonement for sin.

Have a detailed prayer structure. They are obligated to pray five times a day and the prayers are set out already with set movements.	Jesus taught us to pray to our Father, so the relationship that Christians have with God is much more relational, rather than set out and memorised rituals. *Matthew 6:9-13 NIV* *This, then, is how you should pray:* *"Our Father in heaven, hallowed be your name, your kingdom come, your will be done, on earth as it is in heaven. Give us today our daily bread. And forgive us our debts, as we also have forgiven our debtors. And lead us not into temptation, but deliver us from the evil one."*
Salvation is not an assurance but is only dependent on the mercy of Allah.	Salvation is given through Jesus alone. It is assured and completely free. *Romans 10:13 NIV* *Everyone who calls on the name of the Lord shall be saved.*

Do not be afraid to share your faith with Muslims, they have a great understanding of Christian theology. Share the simple, incredible grace of God. Share about how salvation can be found in Jesus alone and share your testimony to back that up!

SOURCES

https://en.wikipedia.org/wiki/Islam

https://en.wikipedia.org/wiki/Christianity_and_
Islam#:~:text=Christianity%20believes%20Jesus%20
to%20be,not%20the%20son%20of%20God.

https://billygraham.org/story/how-can-you-share-the-
gospel-with-muslims/

https://www.thegospelcoalition.org/article/how-to-share-
the-gospel-with-muslims/

https://www.namb.net/apologetics/resource/comparison-
chart-islam-and-christianity/

HOW TO KNOW JESUS
BY COLIN URQUHART

After you have had that conversation with someone and they have prayed the prayer of salvation, they will probably want to know more! Following is a resource – written by my dear friend Pastor Colin Urquhart – that will help you explain the next steps someone who has just given their life to Jesus can take that will help them to understand what a relationship with Jesus is.

You can order these books individually to carry around with you in your car or bag, or in bulk to distribute to a small group or church: **kingdomfaith.com/shop/minibooks.aspx**

How to know Jesus

written by Colin Urquhart

1. WHAT IS A CHRISTIAN?

Ask this question and you will receive a variety of answers, many of them inaccurate. People have to be free from wrong ideas of what it means to be a Christian before they can appreciate the correct answer! Having asked this question of many, here are a few of the typical answers received:

"A Christian is a good person." That should certainly be the case, if we mean by this a person who seeks to live a good life as a good citizen. However, that could be said of many people who definitely would not want to claim they are Christians. In this sense you could have a good atheist, a good humanist, or Buddhist or a follower of any other religion.

"A Christian is someone who goes to church." This would be true of Christians; they do "go to church." However, going to church does not make a person a Christian! Many people go to church, either occasionally or even regularly and are not necessarily Christians.

"A Christian is someone who prays." This should certainly be the case. But many people who are definitely not Christians pray to their 'gods.' The followers of all religions pray in some form or other.

"A Christian is someone who does good deeds." Again this should be true of any Christian believer. But, good deeds

*are not confined to Christians. So the fact that someone
does good deeds for others does not make him or her a
Christian.*

*"A Christian is someone who believes in God." This also
would be true of a Christian, but others who are not
Christians believe in God in some form. Jewish people
believe in the same God as Christians, but most of them
would not claim to be Christians!*

We could continue with many such statements. One thing
is common to all these answers. They all suggest that Christians
are people who do certain things: They seek to live good lives,
they participate in church services, they pray, they do good
deeds, they believe in God. Yet not one of these activities makes
a person a Christian. There are no activities that can make
someone a Christian.

The truth is that a Christian is someone for whom God
has done something. Only God Himself can make a person a
Christian. As a Christian the believer will engage in certain
activities, but none of these activities can make a person a
Christian!

So we will need to understand what God has done already
that will enable people to become Christians. We will also
have to discover what their response is to be to what He has
done!

2. WHY WE WERE CREATED

Humankind is the pinnacle of God's creation; He kept the best until last! This is because He wanted to bring into being a creature that would reflect His own character, a being made in His image. God is a spiritual being. So He created man with a spirit; this is what marks people off from every other creature on earth. His intention was that men and women would be able to have fellowship with Him – spirit to spirit. He wants to reveal His nature to them, but also to share Himself with those He had created.

Because by definition God is perfect, without sin, He first created man perfect, innocent, without sin. The story of Adam and Eve shows how before they were guilty of sin, they were able to have fellowship with God in the garden paradise in which He had placed them.

Sadly this innocence did not last. First, Eve was deceived by the devil and then Adam chose to sin. Eve had lost her perfection when she was deceived, and Adam made the fateful decision to join Eve in her imperfection, instead of remaining true to God. He had a choice between the imperfection of Eve, or the perfection of God.

When Adam made that wrong decision, He immediately lost his innocence, his fellowship and unity with God. Now he was a sinner. Having disobeyed the command God had given him not to eat of the fruit of the tree of good and evil, he felt guilt and shame for the first time, and tried to hide from God as a result. Now the purpose for which He had created man had been frustrated.

As a consequence of this disobedience, Adam and Eve were excluded from the garden paradise. When they lost their innocence, they not only lost their relationship with God, but they also lost their place in paradise! They had tasted evil and were barred from re-entering the garden paradise. And so they lost access to the tree of life, of eternal life, of God's life, that was in the garden.

This exclusion from the garden demonstrated God's judgment on sin. This had such far-reaching consequences that it had to be judged and condemned by God! Intended to live in unity with God, sinners were now outcasts!

3. NOT THE END OF THE STORY

God had created human beings in love. Because His nature is to love; everything He does, He does in love! Despite their sin and failure, God wanted to restore them to fellowship with Him. He wanted to remove their guilt and the judgment and condemnation that guilt deserved! For instead of the perfect nature for which God created man, now every successive generation would be born with a sinful nature with a disposition like that of Adam, choosing to please self rather than to please God! Their sin had resulted in spiritual death, separation from God, instead of living in unity with Him!

In His fore-knowledge God knew that Adam and Eve would fall from grace, and so He had a plan to undo the wrong they had done. First, He gave His people, Israel, a series of commands called 'The law.' These commands they constantly failed to keep, because they had inherited Adam's sinful nature. There were times when Israel truly wanted to obey, and other times when they had no desire to do what God wanted. But even with their best efforts they constantly failed to keep the Lord's commands!

God was demonstrating that it was impossible to obey Him, to please Him and to live in fellowship with Him with this sinful nature - no matter how much people tried to do this. So God had a plan that would enable people to be restored to fellowship, to relationship with Him. There was nothing men and women could do to achieve this, so God would have to take matters into His own hands. He would have to do for His people what they could not accomplish themselves! They could only be restored to unity with Him if He was to deal with their sinful nature and give them a new nature instead, a spiritual nature; His own nature in them!

How could He achieve such a miraculous plan? What would it take to replace that sinful nature with His own nature so that His people could have an entirely different relationship with Him as their Father? He decided to adopt people so they could become His children. To accomplish this they would need to be born again! Their natural birth made each person one of the people He had created. Their second birth would transform their lives and bring them into a Father/child relationship with Him.

How did He achieve this? Humanly it was impossible, but with God nothing is impossible! Such a situation required a radical answer. This God provided through the life, death, and resurrection of His own Son. In Jesus God came into this sinful world, lived a life of perfect obedience to His Father, and then offered His life in sacrifice on behalf of all sinners. Without that sacrifice nobody could be born again, be restored to unity with God and to the heavenly paradise which He intended for His people. So we need to understand why Jesus needed to die on a Cross, and what this accomplished for the whole of sinful mankind.

4. THE VICTORY OF THE CROSS

God is holy, perfect, and complete in Himself. For anyone to be at one with Him, he or she would have to be made totally acceptable to Him. Sin separates people from God; it forms a kind of barrier between God and man. That barrier would have to be removed, otherwise it would be impossible for anyone to relate to Him personally.

Because it has such dire consequences, God could not shrug His shoulders and say that sin did not matter. His righteous judgment upon sinners, those who choose to sin, is that they deserve death, to be eternally separated from Him. However, in His love for those who form part of His creation, He did not want such a judgment to befall them!

This means that God needed to produce a way in which all the sins of sinful humanity could be forgiven, completely removed from the lives of sinners in such a way that it would seem that they had never sinned in the first place! This would make them sinless, blameless before Him. Then they could be made totally acceptable to Him and could enter into a relationship of being one with Him in His love and power!

The extent of such a plan is staggering in itself. The fact that God has already succeeded in fulfilling this plan is a testimony to His love and power. The whole plan is centred around the person of Jesus!

No sinner could remove the sin and guilt of other sinners! This could only be accomplished by someone who was without sin Himself. As the whole of humanity had been born with a sinful nature He would have to become man Himself if He was to achieve His objective.

Before His birth Jesus was the Word that proceeded from the mouth of God. When God spoke creation into being, the Word that went out of His mouth to accomplish this was Jesus. This Word would become a human being. Then it would be possible for those who had previously no relationship with God, to be able to hear His voice and receive teaching about the truth.

To fulfill His plan Jesus would have to be thoroughly human. He was coming to share the weakness of our humanity, to be tempted in the ways in which we are tempted, but without falling into sin! So Jesus had a human nature, but not a sinful nature.

God caused Him to be conceived in the womb of a virgin by His own Spirit, the Holy Spirit. So through Mary He had a human nature; through the Holy Spirit He had a divine nature! He was both thoroughly human and yet with a God nature!

The fact that He was born as a little Child and not a conquering king shows the full extent to which He shared in our humanity. For thirty years He lived in obscurity, waiting for the time when His heavenly Father would enable Him to begin His ministry on the earth.

Jesus had to wait for the Father's commission, because in sharing in our humanity He made it clear that He could initiate nothing Himself to reveal the nature of God's heavenly Kingdom from which He had come. Although He was the Word of God made human, He would only speak what the Father gave Him to speak. He would only do what He saw His Father doing; what the Father was instructing

Him to do. He had to live in complete dependence and obedience to His Father.

Because He shared our humanity completely, He had a human will. But because He also had a God nature, He desired to fulfill the will of the heavenly Father. He understood that He had to do this perfectly. He made it clear that He had not come to earth to pursue any will of His own, but to fulfill the will of His Father in heaven. This meant He had to live in perfect submission to the authority and will of His Father.

His ministry began when He was thirty years old. He came to the River Jordan where a prophetic preacher called John was baptising people, to signify the washing away of their sins. Because Jesus was without sin He did not need to be baptised. He chose to do so because He was identifying totally with the sinful humanity He had come to save from an eternity lived in Hell, in complete separation from God.

When He came up out of the water, the power of the Holy Spirit came upon Jesus as He was praying, to equip Him for His ministry that was now to begin. A voice was heard from Heaven, proclaiming Jesus to be God's Son, the long-awaited Messiah or Christ.

Jesus began to teach the people about the Kingdom of Heaven, the Kingdom of God. Both titles can be used interchangeably. He made it clear that God wanted to make His Kingdom available to all who turned to Jesus with repentance and faith, to give them this Kingdom as a gift! There was no way that anyone could earn such a gift by their own works. No matter what they did, their works would never free them from the sinful nature that separated them from God. They could never do anything to deserve such a wonderful gift. They could only become part of the heavenly Kingdom by the grace of God alone, by His free gift to them, despite the fact that they deserved to receive nothing from Him!

Jesus wanted to give this gift to those who believed in Him and chose to follow Him. They needed faith to believe that there was nothing they could do themselves to accomplish acceptance from God and His desire to save them from the consequences of their sinful nature. They would have to trust Jesus alone to save them, to become their Saviour. To accomplish this they would need to repent as well as believe.

This repentance is in two parts. First of all their sins have to be forgiven, for God cannot become one with sinners, but only with those who have been freed from the consequences of their sins. Second, they would need to surrender their lives to God so that He would be the Lord of their lives.

Such repentance and faith would enable people to receive the new birth, the second birth, the heavenly birth. They would be born again and be given a new nature, a divine nature so, like Jesus, they would become totally acceptable to God and able to live at one with Him, sharing in His divine life. Without this new birth, Jesus made clear that people would not be able to see the Kingdom of God, let alone become part of this heavenly Kingdom! They had to be born again!

Their natural birth had given them a human nature; their new birth would give them a God nature, a divine nature. In other words, Jesus would not only be with them but would come to live in them by the power of His Spirit!

We are beginning to see how far reaching and radical God's plan was that was being fulfilled through His Son Jesus.

But why was it necessary for Him to die on a Cross for the outworking of His commission from the Father, to make it possible for all who repent and believe to become part of His heavenly Kingdom? Could He not simply have taught people about the Kingdom and asked them to become His followers?

No, Jesus had to be crucified because God is just! His judgment on sin had to be executed, literally! Death was God's just and righteous judgment on all sins, whether big or small, because any sin has this dire consequence of separating people from knowing God personally!

If a sinner was to die for other sinners this would not eradicate their sin, or the judgment that they deserved as sinners. However, if someone who is without sin took the judgment sinners deserved upon himself, then this would free them from the death they deserved. Jesus was the only One who could achieve this. However, because He was sinless, innocent of any guilt or sin, He did not deserve to die, so He had to make His life a willing sacrifice made on behalf of all sinners. The crucifixion demonstrates the judgment we all deserve, and that Jesus never deserved! He took upon Himself the punishment that should have been ours!

But if He had to die for us, why on a Cross, the most painful form of death? Could He not have been run through with a sword, or killed in some other way? No, He had to die the death of a condemned criminal, even though He Himself was innocent. Pilate, who condemned Him to death, knew He was innocent and was reluctant to condemn Him! But Jesus had surrendered Himself to His accusers because He knew what His death would accomplish. He took upon Himself the condemnation that we deserve because we have all sinned and have grieved God in the process!

This demonstrates the mercy and love that God has for us. We deserve nothing from Him. Yet in His love for us, He sends His Son to die the death of a condemned criminal for us! As a result, all our sins can be forgiven, because Jesus has already paid the penalty that our sins deserve.

So the punishment of all sinners of every generation was laid on Jesus. They could be set free from the guilt and punishment they deserved, and be made totally acceptable to God. Then they would become His children by virtue of the fact that they had received the new life He came to make it possible for them to receive!

Once you are born again you are no longer a sinner with a sinful nature that rules your life, determining the decisions you make, the way you think, and what you choose to say and do! You are given a new nature that will enable you to know God personally as your Father and to live in ways that please Him rather than grieve Him.

5. EVEN MORE RADICAL

However, the way for God to make it possible for believers to live at one with Him was even more radical than simply sending His Son to die for them. He wanted to provide a solution to the conflict that would inevitably arise between the old life, that was bound by sin, and the new life imparted by God's Spirit.

God's purpose was not to try and improve the old life; that would be impossible. You cannot improve the sinful nature. No, His intention was to replace the old life with an entirely new life. Not improvement, but replacement! So the old life would have to die before the new birth could take place!

Now we can understand more of the radical nature of the Cross. Not only did Jesus die for us and for all sinners, but He took us to the Cross with Him. All of sinful humanity was present in the crucifixion! So the Scriptures affirm clearly that we are crucified with Christ, because it was our punishment that He was taking upon Himself.

The apostle Paul said: "I have been crucified with Christ and I no longer live, but Christ lives in me." At the time of the crucifixion Paul (or Saul as he was then) was not a follower of Jesus. But when he became a Christian, he understood that his new life had only been made possible because Jesus had taken the person he used to be to the Cross with Him. So when Jesus died, Saul of Tarsus died with Him, not physically but spiritually speaking. This enabled him to become the new person who had been born again and who became one of the greatest followers of Jesus. Paul wrote about one third of the New Testament.

So you are able to say that you were crucified with Christ. The person you were no longer exists once you have been born again. You then become a new creation, a brand new person, with the Spirit of Jesus Christ living within you.

You sometimes hear people say that if they could start their lives all over again they would not make the same mistakes as they did in the past. This seems wishful thinking; yet this is precisely what Jesus has made possible! The new birth means precisely that: A new beginning has taken place!

Now it is clear from the Bible that when people have put their faith in Jesus and have been born again, they should then be baptised in water. John the Baptist had been baptising people for the forgiveness of their sins. To be baptised as a Christian was noticeably more significant. It was the funeral service of the old life! Going into the water and being submerged signifies that the old life has died and has been buried, finished with forever! When the newly baptised believer comes up out of the water, he or she does so as a new creation. The old has gone and the new has come! The new believer can now live a new life.

However, God knows that this new Christian will need to be empowered to follow Him, and to be able to live this new life. No matter how hard a person can try to fulfill the will of God, this is impossible by depending on his or her own natural life. To live the life that will please God can only be lived by God Himself living in us.

When Jesus came up out of the water after His baptism, God's Spirit came upon Him as He was praying. The Spirit of God, the life and power of God, was given to Him for the outworking of His ministry. Jesus could now fulfil His purpose as the Christ, the Messiah, meaning the Anointed One.

God's purpose is to anoint you with His Holy Spirit, for the Holy Spirit of God to be imparted to you, to live within you to enable you to live the new life, not in your own strength, but in His!

The Holy Spirit is the Spirit, the life, and power of God, of Jesus Christ; and He will come to live in you to empower you to live this new life. You will not have to strive to please Him by depending upon yourself. Instead you will be able to depend on the life of His Spirit within you! Christ in you, the hope of glory! This wonderful gift to you will enable you to please the Lord by the way He enables you to fulfill His will for your life!

He is not only prepared to save you from the old life of sin, failure, and self-dependence. He desires to give you a brand new life with the person of Jesus Christ actually within you by the power of His Spirit! He wants you to live full of His Spirit that is so much more powerful than your natural human life. Christ in you, expressing His life in and through you, not as an end in itself, but so the life of God's Son can flow out of your life, causing you to become a blessing to many people!

6. THE HOLY SPIRIT

When you give your life to Jesus, He gives His life to you. That is a great trade in! It is like trading in a rusty old car and receiving in return a brand new Rolls Royce without any cost to yourself, except letting go of the old car! Jesus has paid the price for you through His sacrifice on the Cross, making it possible for you to be born again, and to receive the new life of His Spirit.

Your natural birth gave you your human nature, which sadly is a sinful nature; your new birth gives you a new nature, God's nature, to live in you! What an amazing gift! When you are born again you are given this new nature; and as with Jesus, God wants your life to be full of the Spirit. Then you can live daily in the power of His Spirit, not relying solely on your human life and power!

So we need to understand the nature of this wonderful gift, and what practical effects this gift is to have on your life.

The Holy Spirit is God. The Bible speaks of the three persons of God, the three ways in which the one and only God has chosen to reveal Himself to us: As the Father who loves us, the Son who gave His life to save us, and as the Holy Spirit of God who lives within us. So the Holy Spirit is the Spirit of both God the Father and God the Son.

The Holy Spirit is the person, the life, and the power of God given to live in you to enable you to fulfill God's will for your life! The Lord knows you could never please Him with your old sinful nature, no matter how hard you tried! It is a remarkable sign of God's love for you that He should want to come and live in you in the person of His Spirit; this is the mercy and grace of God, His desire to give you everything, although you deserve nothing!

Because He is the person of God, the Spirit shares the same characteristics as the Father and the Son. He wants to reproduce these in your life, so that your new life reveals the character of Jesus, just as He revealed the character of His Father during His earthly ministry. This does not happen by you trying to imitate Jesus, but by allowing the life of His Spirit in you to be expressed in your life.

Paul speaks of these qualities of the Holy Spirit's life in you as the fruit of the Holy Spirit. He describes this fruit as consisting of God's love, joy, peace, patience, kindness, goodness, faithfulness, gentleness, and self-control. One fruit with nine flavours! When you consider this list you realise that you would like to see more of these qualities in your life, that your life would be much richer and more satisfying if this was the case. You can see also that others who know you would like to see more of these qualities in you! Most important of all, God wants to produce more of these qualities in your life.

The Holy Spirit is the Spirit of love, enabling you to love God with all your heart, and to love others as He has loved you. He will even enable you to love your enemies!

The love of the Holy Spirit is not like human love that is based on emotion or desire. God's love is always constant, no matter how you feel or what circumstances you are faced with. It is a love that is expressed in giving, out of a desire for the welfare of those who are the object of this love. It is with such love that God loves you. He wants to give more and more of Himself to you out of His concern for your welfare.

He is the Spirit of joy. His joy is much greater than human happiness that depends upon our response to what we experience. Like His love, God's joy is always consistent. You will be able to rejoice in the Lord, even in the midst of the most trying of circumstances, because Jesus is much greater than any problem that you could ever face. When you rejoice in Him, you proclaim His victory over your difficulties!

He is the Spirit of peace. God's peace is described as being "beyond our understanding." This peace gives you a deep and satisfied sense of well-being. We are then at peace with God and with ourselves. This enables us also to be at peace with others, even when there may be difficult relationships to cope with.

Many would admit to needing more patience. As this is a quality of God's Spirit, to need more patience indicates a need for more of God's Spirit to be revealed in a person's life.

The more you live in dependence upon God, the more all these qualities will be expressed in your life, including that of self-control!

The self-life is the old life centred on pleasing self, an essentially selfish and sinful life! Once you have the new life of the Holy Spirit you can choose to deny any temptation to go back to the old life, living to please yourself, for you are empowered by God's presence within you to live the new life that pleases Him. Jesus said that anyone who follows Him will have to deny their old self to do this; for then the Holy Spirit will express His life in and through you.

Paul describes these qualities as fruit because they grow in you as long as you continue to live in relationship with God.

He is the Spirit of Truth who guides you into the truth of who God is, of what He has accomplished for you through

Jesus, and how He enables you to fulfil His will through the power of the Holy Spirit within you. He is your Counsellor, the one who becomes the voice of God within you. He reminds you of what Jesus has said, and is always ready to speak words of faith to your heart, words that are most relevant to your situation! He enables you to have God's wisdom so that you know what to do and what decisions to make.

Jesus taught that the Holy Spirit does not act independently of the Father and the Son. When the Holy Spirit speaks into your heart, it is the Father and the Son speaking. For there is always complete unity between the Father, Son, and the Holy Spirit. When you become a child of God, He wants to lead and guide you in the way He wants you to go!

Jesus promised the disciples that they would receive God's power when they were filled with the Holy Spirit. This same promise applies to every believer today. So when you receive the gift of God's Spirit you will receive His supernatural power, which is so much greater than the natural human power that you already possess. You are empowered by God Himself to fulfill His will for your life.

The new life is a gift from God. The Kingdom of Heaven is a gift to you; and the Holy Spirit is His gift to enable you to live as one who belongs to His Kingdom!

He is the Spirit of power. This Kingdom is not a matter of talk, something we can simply speak about, but of power, God's power! The Kingdom of God is, "Righteousness, peace, and joy in the Holy Spirit." So the power of the Holy Spirit enables you to live the life of God's Kingdom here on earth. Jesus will enable you to rule over your circumstances rather than to think of yourself as a victim of your circumstances! It is amazing to think that God is ready to make such power available to you! But He does this only when you have surrendered your life to Him; He does not want to put such power into the wrong hands! This is not power to be used only for yourself, but to enable you to fulfill His purpose for you to love others as He has loved you!

The New Testament speaks of a number of different ways in which this power is expressed in the lives of believers in very practical ways. We will not speak at length about these now, for it is not possible to see how such things can take place in your life until you have received the gift of the Spirit yourself. Then these different manifestations of the Spirit will become available to you. It is enough to say here that God gives you knowledge when you lack it, wisdom when you need it, prophetic words to encourage you, and will even give healings and miracles in response to your faith as a believer!

The Holy Spirit is the Spirit of faith. He inspires faith in the hearts of Christians, even when previously there was a complete lack of faith. The way He does this is by speaking words of truth into your heart, words of Scripture that are appropriate to you at that particular time. Hearing God in this way inspires faith!

All these different ways in which the Spirit will work in your life point to the fact that you will never be alone; that He is always with you, ready to work within you. He will never leave you to your own devices. He will not only be with you always; He will be within you ready to express His life of love and power through you. Jesus is described as the Author and Perfector of our faith. By His Spirit He will speak words of faith to your heart. When you believe Him and act on those words, His supernatural life and power will be released into your situation.

He is also the Spirit of worship and of prayer. He will fill your worship with His presence and the power of God. He makes your prayer in the Name of Jesus both powerful and effective. In fact, He will enrich your life in so many ways. You will have the option of trusting in yourself or in the Spirit of God within you; of doing things in your own strength or in His power!

7. THE BODY OF CHRIST

When you give your life to Jesus so many wonderful things take place. God takes hold of you and places you into Christ. To enable the disciples to understand what this means, Jesus used a vivid illustration when speaking to them at the Last Supper that took place on the evening before His crucifixion.

Jesus described Himself as the True Vine. All the disciples were familiar in seeing vines growing. A vine consists of a root system, the main stem, the branches of that stem, and the fruit, the grapes that grow on the branches. Because Jesus is the Vine, He is the whole plant.

He likened the disciples to the branches of this Vine. So they live in this Vine. In Jesus! The heavenly Father is the One who tends the Vine, to ensure that it is exceedingly fruitful. So He cuts out of the Vine any branches that do not bear fruit, those who simply want to draw life out of the Vine but do nothing to serve the One in whom they live. Even the fruitful branches the Father prunes so that they will continue to bear more fruit. It is necessary to prune a natural vine every year so that the new growth will produce new fruit!

The fruit gives glory and honour to the Father because this is fulfilling the will and purpose He has for the branches. So God the Father takes hold of your life when you give yourself to Him, so that for the rest of your life you will be able to draw life everyday from Jesus, and produce the fruit that will please the Father, giving you a tremendous sense of fulfillment and satisfaction! You will not need to fear being cut out of the Vine, for to remain in Him will enable the sap of the Holy Spirit to flow through your life and produce the fruit. The lasting fruit is produced by the life and power of the Holy Spirit, God's precious gift in you.

Paul used another vivid illustration to describe the life you will have as a believer in Jesus Christ. He described believers in Him as being part of the Body of Christ. This is a good description of born again people.

In a human body there are many different parts. They all work together for the good, the welfare, the health of the whole body. Each part has its distinctive functions: The eye to see, the ear to hear, the mouth to speak, the heart to beat, the leg to walk and so on. Each individual believer is like one part of this body. That part does not have to try to be like other parts; it simply has to fulfill the particular function it has for the health of the whole body. The eye want to be a good eye, not an ear!

This can seem obvious but it points to an important truth. When you place your faith in Jesus, God places you in this Body because He has a particular purpose for you. You will have an important contribution to make for the life and well-being of the whole Body. Nobody else can fulfill the part God intends you to play because the other parts are occupied in fulfilling their own distinctive purposes!

So God's purpose for your life will be fulfilled within this context of living in His Body. The Blood of Jesus will continue to flow through your life to ensure that you are forgiven and made fit for use. The life of God's Spirit will continue to flow through your life to equip and enable you to fulfill that purpose!

Of course, there are certain things that every member of

the Body does to remain spiritually healthy. Every member is called to develop his or her relationship with Jesus through prayer. This is not a matter of repeating formal prayers, for when you know Jesus personally you will be able to speak to Him freely from your heart. You will also be able to hear from Him through His Spirit and through the words of Scripture in particular.

Every member is called by God to love the other members of the Body so that the whole Body can function together in unity. It is amazing to see how this works in the natural human body. The same principle is to be seen working in the Body of Christ! This can only be the case when each of the members of the Body is not concerned only about his or her own welfare, but is equally concerned about all the other members of the Body to which he or she belongs. This is why when God gives you the precious gift of the Holy Spirit He fills your heart and life with His love, the love that is consistent and faithful, that does not change with emotion and circumstances. The love that is concerned about the welfare of others. The love that is expressed in giving and serving others, in encouraging them and whenever necessary being merciful to them; forgiving them instead of taking offence if they do anything that offends you!

This Body exists to be God's instrument in causing His life to flow out of the Body to touch the lives of others living in the world. Those who are living in spiritual darkness are able to receive the light of the life of Jesus Christ that will transform their lives, giving them an eternal destiny in the Kingdom of Heaven.

Jesus Christ is the Head of this Body. It is from the head in a natural body that all the limbs take their direction. When you choose to move your arm something is taking place in your head that is transmitted through the various parts of your body between the head and the arm, enabling the movement to take place. The arm needs to be in relationship with the head and with the other parts of the body; otherwise there will be paralysis and the movement will not take place.

Jesus is the Head and He wants to direct your life as part of His Body. He wants you to be in good relationship with Him and with the other members of the Body of Christ. There is no such thing as an independent Christian who does not belong to the Body, just as there cannot be a fruitful branch of the Vine unless it remains attached to the rest of the Vine!

The new commandment that Jesus gave to go with the new life that He was enabling believers to receive, is to love one another as Jesus has loved us. He loved us to the extent of laying down His life for us. In the same way, we are to love one another by living for one another, not simply for ourselves.

This is yet another wonderful truth, for to be part of the Body of Christ means that you belong to a group of people who are devoted to you for your welfare, just as you are devoted to them for their welfare. We can all love, support, and care for one another in the ways that are appropriate in the various situations in which we find ourselves.

8. THE CHURCH

The True Vine and the Body of Christ are both biblical descriptions of what God intends for His church. Now here we have to face some uncomfortable facts, for the church does not always appear to be what God intends. The church is to be the assembly or gathering together of groups of people who have been born again, have this new life of the Spirit, and are filled with the life and power of God. People who love one another with God's love, and are therefore seeking the welfare of all who belong to the Body, so that the church may fulfill the purposes of God in the world. This is to bring more and more people into the life of God's Kingdom so they can enjoy all the blessings and benefits of this Kingdom, not only in this life but for all eternity!

God never intended His church to become an institution where people only meet together for a series of religious services. He did not come to start yet another formal religion; He came with the precious gift of God's Kingdom and the empowering of the Holy Spirit to enable people to live the life of this Kingdom here on earth!

Sadly, the experience of church for many who are not yet filled with the new life is one of formal, often boring services that do not seem to be particularly relevant to the circumstances of their lives. Instead of finding that their experience draws them to a living relationship with Jesus Christ, the very opposite seems to be the case. In some churches it is clear that the truth of God's Word is not preached with faith, and the participants do not seem to radiate the life of which the gospels speaks!

It is good that this is not a description of all assemblies, for there are churches where the Word of God is preached and believed, where the members radiate the life and love of Jesus. Where the worship is filled with the power of God's Spirit, His presence there can be discerned, even by visitors who do not know the Lord. These churches radiate the light of God's Kingdom, not only because they meet on Sundays, but because the members are intent on living as true disciples. Their activities during the week are as important as their assemblies on Sundays. Each member is being encouraged to develop his or her particular calling from God. Obviously new believers need to become part of an assembly or local church that seeks to be a biblical expression of the Body of Christ, a church where they will be fed with the truth, encouraged in their faith and receive the love and support they need as new Christians. In such an environment they will soon discover the particular purpose God has for their lives, and they will be able to receive from God the anointing they need to be able to fulfill those purposes!

It is important to realise that in giving yourself to Jesus you are committing yourself to becoming a member of the Body of Christ, with all that this implies. In His tender love and compassion, God will lead you step by step in the way He wants you to go. He knows you will thrive spiritually by being part of a local expression of His Body that is vibrant with His life, and where the people are dedicated to God's Kingdom purposes. In such a context you will be loved and accepted, and will come to love and accept all the others who form part of this assembly!

It is not God's intention for you to judge any church that does not seem to fulfill what God intends. Rather you will want to pray for a movement of God's Spirit to breathe the new life of His Spirit into every congregation, regardless of any denomination and affiliation!

What the Lord has in store for you as a member of His Body is a life of knowing that God is pleased by the fruit He is able to produce in your life through the life and power of His Spirit. He wants to place alongside you other believers who will help and encourage you so that, in due course, you will be able to help and encourage others. As a result God will be blessed and honoured in your life, not only by the praises you sing, but by the life you live!

9. WHAT NOW?

How can the life of God's Kingdom become a reality in your life and experience? How can you not only be born again, but also filled with the life of God's Spirit? How can your life be filled with love for God and for others? How can you be confident that He will fulfill the plans and purposes God has for your life? How can you be blessed because you live daily in a living relationship with Jesus, a relationship in which you will experience answered prayer?

You may never go to church or be part of a congregation at present. It may be that you have been part of a formal church that does not seem to radiate the life which we have been describing. Maybe that you consider your life to have been so sinful that God would want nothing to do with you, that you could never become acceptable to Him.

No matter what your present situation, the way forward is the same for everyone as Jesus made clear: Repentance and faith! So how can you put this into practice? How can you repent? What do you need to do to express faith in Jesus?

There follows a simple way in which all these questions can be answered. Countless numbers of people have done what I am about to suggest to you, and to great affect in their lives. People have been born again, filled with God's Spirit and have often received healing from God by using this simple method. In other words, experience has proved that it works!

Write a letter to Jesus. This letter will be in two parts. First, write down all the things for which you are conscious of needing forgiveness. It is important not only to think about these things, but to write them down for reasons that will become clear.

This does not suggest that you are to remember every sin. If that was the case you would need to write a book, not a letter! There will be things that you are conscious of immediately for which you recognize your need of forgiveness, things for which you feel guilty every time something happens to trigger the memory of those things. These are the things that if you could have your life over again you would never choose to repeat! God wants to free you from all the shame and guilt attached to these events. So write them down. You can say to God in this letter: "Lord, help me to remember now anything that has had a negative impact on my life, so You can free me from the consequences of these sins." You will find that certain things will come to mind as a result. Write them down.

You can begin your letter by saying: "Lord Jesus, I am giving You my life and I ask You to forgive anything that has been opposed to Your will." Then begin to list the sins and offenses that God will forgive.

Obviously you will need to set a time apart when you can do this thoughtfully and sincerely. However, you will find that this begins a process and during the following days you will become conscious of further things you need to add to the letter. I usually suggest that this is written over a period of a week or so. When you return to the letter it will only be for a short time to add the further things for which you need God's forgiveness.

Why write these things down? For this reason. You can think of one thing after another, but it is only when you see them written down that you can see what a sorry mess that your life has been spiritually! You will see not that it is a good idea to seek God's forgiveness, but that you have a desperate need of His forgiveness so that you can come into the place of knowing that you are totally forgiven and made completely acceptable to God as a result.

In the second part of your letter write down all that you are giving to God. He wants to become Lord in every part of your life. Wherever He is Lord there will be blessing and fulfillment. So you can say: "Lord, I am giving You my life"; then be specific. Offer Him your heart, your soul life, that is your mind, your emotions and your will. Offer Him your body so that every area of your life can be used for His glory. Offer Him your relationships, your family and your friends, your work life and your leisure life. Surrender your natural gifts to Him so that they can be used for His glory. Give Him your future, your money, your property. This is not because He wants to take away from you. The very opposite is the case, for Jesus stated clearly that God will always give back to you far more than you can give to Him. He will give you, "Good measure, pressed down, shaken together, and running over." But He can only multiply what has first been put into His hands.

Again, during subsequent days you will become conscious of further ways in which you will need to surrender yourself to the Lordship of Jesus Christ. Add these to the letter. It is better to keep the two parts of the letter on separate sheets of paper so you can add the future sins that need to be forgiven on one sheet, and the further ways in which you need to give your life to Him on the other.

You might have heard of others coming to Christ in a more superficial way than this. I am telling you the thorough way that will enable you to have a meaningful relationship of love with Jesus and become a true disciple. So the more thorough you are, the better!

Once you are confident that your letter is complete, what are you to do with it? You will need to set a time apart to speak it out aloud to Jesus. You can do this on your own. If you know a pastor, or devoted Christian who you can trust, you may choose to do this while they are present. The advantage of this is the person can give you the assurance of God's forgiveness and then pray for you to be filled with the Holy Spirit.

However, if such a person is not available you can do this on your own, and the Lord will surely hear your prayer and will answer you. I have never known of anyone who has written such a letter to Jesus who has not been greatly blessed as a result.

During the first part of your letter it will be important to forgive any who you need to forgive because of the ways they have betrayed you or hurt you by the things they have said about you or done to you. Jesus makes it clear that if we expect God to be merciful to us and to forgive us, we need to be merciful to others and forgive them. He said: "Blessed are the merciful for they shall obtain mercy!"

Once you have spoken your letter to Jesus destroy the first part. All these sins will have been forgiven and no longer exist. So burn it or tear it into small shreds and dispose of it. You will never need to visit any of these things again. You may remember some of them from time to time, but there will no longer be any guilt or shame attached to them!

Beware of the enemy. The devil is the accuser who tries to encourage people to feel condemned. He doesn't want to let you go from his influence so that for the rest of your life you will be under the influence of the Holy Spirit. If ever he tries to accuse you of things you have done in the past that have been forgiven you can say to him: "Satan, I am forgiven and there is no condemnation for me because I belong to Jesus, which is more than can be said for you! So goodbye!" He is under condemnation and will never belong to Jesus!

You can keep the second part of the letter in a safe place. If you choose to do this, you can return to it every so often to remind yourself of what you have surrendered to Jesus. Sometimes we tend to take back what we have given, and this reminder helps us remedy that temptation!

When you have read your letter to Jesus, ask Him to fill you with His life, the life and power of His Holy Spirit. Jesus said that all who ask receive. The heavenly Father gives the Holy Spirit to those who ask Him. You will have a sense of peace that you are now forgiven and accepted by God. You may feel truly joyful and liberated. You may simply have the sense that all is now well between God and yourself.

When the Spirit of God comes upon you, there may be a sense of joyful release taking place within you. However, do not measure your experience against what you hear others have experienced. God deals with each one of us personally and in the right way for each one. Jesus told us to believe that we have received whatever we ask when we pray. So thank Him for the precious gift of His Spirit, regardless of any feelings or experiences you may or may not have.

You may have been told by someone that when you receive the gift of the Holy Spirit that God gives you another language with which to pray, one which you do not understand yourself. Such a gift enables the Holy Spirit to pray in you and through you in a way which is beyond your understanding! So, as with all the gifts of the Holy Spirit, this is a very precious and useful gift. However, do not be discouraged if you do not manifest this gift immediately. Simply thank God that He has answered your prayer and He has given you His Spirit and that you will, in due course be able to speak and pray in this other language.

You will certainly find that a number of significant things have changed in your life, whether you speak in tongues immediately or not. Every one of these is evidence of the new life of the Spirit that is now active in your life!

Even if you have spoken your letter to Jesus privately, you may want to ask a pastor or friend who has been filled with the Holy Spirit to pray for you with the laying on of hands. This can help you to know that you have received the Lord and the fulfillment of His wonderful promise.

Now you have become a new creation, the old has gone and the new has come! The sinner that you are has died and has been buried with Christ. As you take your place in the local expression of the Body of Christ, you can ask to be baptised, as this is the funeral service of your old life. Now you can live the life of God's Kingdom in the power of the Holy Spirit. Now you can live for the glory of God by fulfilling His purpose for your life as He unfolds this before you.

What a God! What a Saviour! What great mercy and grace! And what a great life you can now live with the expectation that you can reign eternally with Jesus in His heavenly glory! Amen! It shall be so!

Now follow up *Soul Winner* with *Breathe Again*:

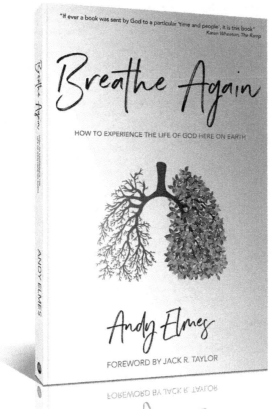

In *Breathe Again* you will learn:

- How God intended for you to breathe, and how you can experience a restoration of that correct breathing today.
- How Eden is no longer a physical place far, far away, but a way of life that everyone who belongs to God can know.
- How to enter into the rest that the Lord has provided for you to know.
- How to exchange a worry-filled life for carefree one.

You'll also receive practical and applicable teaching on how to manage the three parts – spirit, soul and body – of who you are, so you can experience His life in its fullness.

Available from **greatbiglife.co.uk**

About the Author

Andy and his wife Gina are the Senior Pastors of Family Church, a multi-congregational church located on the South Coast of England. Andy is a visionary leader who has grown the church from twelve people on its first day to now being a significant and influential church in the UK and beyond.

Andy is also the founder of Great Big Life a ministry established to see people equipped and empowered not only to lead effectively in Church but also in every other section and sphere of life too.

Andy has a wealth of experience and wisdom to offer that comes from a very successful time in ministry. As well as planting churches, he has been involved in many forms of evangelism including travelling as an evangelist for many years across the United Kingdom and throughout the world.

A dynamic visionary, Andy helps people to see things outside of the box and, as a strategist, he helps others to set goals within their lives and ministries and move towards them quickly. His experience, combined with his life-coaching skills, makes him a valuable asset to any pastor or leader seeking personal development encouragement and to address change.

A highly sought-after conference speaker for events and conferences, Andy regularly shares on a whole range of subjects including spiritual leadership and evangelism. Andy's versatility allows him to communicate as a pastor, an evangelist, a teacher or coach reaching individuals of all ages and in a variety of settings. Andy is very natural and irreligious in his approach, using humour well and being very animated and often unconventional in his delivery. His desire is to lead people to Jesus and help them to discover all that is now available to them through what Jesus has done for them. His personal mandate is 'to know the King and to advance His kingdom.'

Originally from Portsmouth, this is where Andy and Gina, along with their five children, Olivia, Ethan, Gabrielle, Sophie and Christina, now reside and lead the different ministries from.

Useful Links

Keep up-to-date with Andy by connecting with him through his website and social media. Visit:

LINKTR.EE/ANDY.ELMES

to find links to him on social media and his various church and ministry websites.

Also by Andy Elmes

Breakfast of Champions, Volume 1
ISBN: 978-09928027-0-7

Breakfast of Champions, Volume 2
ISBN: 978-09932693-2-5

God's Blueprint for His Church
ISBN: 978-09928027-2-1

The Glass of Water
ISBN: 978-14823513-1-6

iamredemption
ISBN: 978-09928027-4-5

Breath Again
ISBN: 978-19160388-0-6

Available from **greatbiglife.co.uk**

Further Information

For further information about the author of this book, or to order more copies, please contact:

Great Big Life Publishing
Empower Centre
83-87 Kingston Road
Portsmouth
Hants
PO2 7DX
UK

info@greatbiglifepublishing.com
www.greatbiglifepublishing.com
@GBLPublishing

Are you an Author?

Do you have a Word from God on your heart that you're looking to get published to a wider audience? We're looking for manuscripts that identify with our own vision of bringing life-giving and relevant messages to the Body of Christ. Send yours for review towards possible publication to:

Great Big Life Publishing
Empower Centre
83-87 Kingston Road
Portsmouth
Hants
PO2 7DX
UK

or, email us at info@greatbiglifepublishing.com

Are you an Author?